MW00823867

Liturgy and Theology

Liturgy & Theology

ECONOMY AND REALITY

Nathan G. Jennings

CASCADE *Books* • Eugene, Oregon

LITURGY AND THEOLOGY
Economy and Reality

Cascade Books
An Imprint of Wipf and Stock Publishers
199 W. 8th Ave., Suite 3
Eugene, OR 97401
www.wipfandstock.com

PAPERBACK ISBN: 978-1-4982-2930-2
HARDCOVER ISBN: 978-1-4982-2932-6
EBOOK ISBN: 978-1-4982-2931-9

Cataloguing-in-Publication data:

Names: Jennings, Nathan G., 1974–

Title: Liturgy and theology : economy and reality / Nathan G. Jennings.

Description: Eugene, OR: Cascade Books, 2017 | Includes bibliographical references and index.

Identifiers: ISBN 978-1-4982-2930-2 (paperback) | ISBN 978-1-4982-2932-6 (hardcover) | ISBN 978-1-4982-2931-9 (ebook)

Subjects: LCSH: Liturgy, worship, and society | Liturgics | Schmemann, Alexander, 1921–1983 | Theology

Classification: BV176.3 J46 2017 (print) | BV176.3 (ebook)

Manufactured in the U.S.A.

Elements of the following chapters derive from two previously published works, by permission of the publishers: "Contemplating the Mystery: Liturgical Theology as Retrieval of Christian Realism." *Questions Liturgiques* 96, no. 1 (2015). "Divine Economy, Divine Liturgy: Liturgical Theology as a Retrieval of Figural Interpretation," *Radical Orthodoxy: Theology, Philosophy, Politics* 2, no. 1 (2014) 90–117.

Unless otherwise noted, Scripture quotations are from New Revised Standard Version Bible, copyright © 1989 National Council of the Churches of Christ in the United States of America. Used by permission. All rights reserved worldwide. Some Scripture quotations taken from the New American Standard Bible® (NASB), Copyright © 1960, 1962, 1963, 1968, 1971, 1972, 1973, 1975, 1977, 1995 by The Lockman Foundation. Used by permission. www.Lockman.org

To Vitaly and Maria

There may be times when what is most needed is not so much a new discovery or a new idea as a different "slant"; I mean a comparatively slight readjustment in our *way* of looking at the things and ideas on which attention is already fixed.

—OWEN BARFIELD, *SAVING THE APPEARANCES: A STUDY IN IDOLATRY*

Table of Contents

Preface

The epigraph from Owen Barfield, above, recalls the old proverb "he cannot see the forest for the trees." The kind of work that Barfield recommends as sometimes necessary is the work of a landscape painter, not an arborist. In this book, I have followed Barfield's suggestion and example, and tried to step back in order to bring to attention an approach to theology, rather than maintain focus upon the minutiae of given authoritative interpretations. I look to a way in which a more complete reception of Alexander Schmemann's gift of liturgical theology in the West could constitute just such a readjustment in our way of looking at things. Attempting to do so is ambitious at best, and I do so only on the shoulders of giants, who are, chiefly, in this case, Henri de Lubac and Alexander Schmemann. I do so within the Anglican Platonic tradition in which I have over time come to find myself firmly situated.[1] I beg the reader to indulge this work as a bit of landscape painting from which, perhaps, we may retain a worthwhile "leaf."[2]

During my formation in academic theology, I was exposed to de Lubac's amazing contributions. I was persuaded by the unity he maintained between the divine nature, contemplation, and scriptural interpretation. I was especially impressed by his important points about the centrality of the old covenant Scriptures to the very meaning of Christian biblical interpretation, for they simply were what constituted Christian Scripture in our earliest centuries. When I found myself blessed with the position of teaching liturgy at a seminary, I immersed myself in all that I lacked in my new field. I found a new home in liturgical theology. But I was haunted by the lack of engagement with Old Testament exegesis in the wonderful and

1. For a classic description of the Anglican and English tradition of Platonism, see Inge, *The Platonic Tradition* and Douglas Hedley's works.

2. See Tolkien, "Leaf by Niggle."

life-changing works I was discovering. I thus set out on a research trajectory of ritual behavior in the old covenant Scriptures and literary allusions, shapes, and patterns derived from Israel's liturgical life. The following work is the result of my research into the intersection of Scripture, and especially old covenant Scripture, in liturgical theology. This work led me to conclusions that have surprised me. I have become increasingly convinced that if Western Christians are to receive all the gifts liturgical theology has to offer us, then we must accept the kind of metaphysical realism assumed in the approach of its founder, Alexander Schmemann. Our Western academic heritage of unquestioning nominalism slows and confuses our process of reception. Realism makes liturgical theology possible. What began as research into the connection between Old Testament liturgy and ritual allusion led me, interestingly, to recommit to the Platonic stream within the Anglican tradition. I could not have seen that coming.

Some of the content of these chapters derive from two previously published articles and a presentation. "Contemplating the Mystery: Liturgical Theology as Retrieval of Christian Realism" (*Questions Liturgiques* 96, no. 1 [2015]), was first delivered as a presentation at the LEST IX conference, Leuven, 2013. Content from it has contributed to both Chapter Three and the Conclusion. "Divine Economy, Divine Liturgy: Liturgical Theology as a Retrieval of Figural Interpretation" (*Radical Orthodoxy: Theology, Philosophy, Politics*, 2, no. 1 [2014] 90–117) was first delivered to the Liturgical Theology Seminar of the North American Academy of Liturgy, 2012. Content from it has contributed to both Chapter Four and the Conclusion. The core of Chapter Two is "Liturgical Theology and the Sacrifice of Jesus Christ," a presentation delivered to the Liturgical Theology Seminar of the North American Academy of Liturgy, 2013. Please forgive any choppiness or repetition between the chapters. I have done my best to integrate these previous works into a smooth whole. But I have not done so perfectly.

I am thankful for Scott Bader-Saye's discernment of a good publisher for my research and his placing me in contact with Wipf and Stock. I am thankful for the support of the Seminary of the Southwest in terms of a sabbatical for the Spring semester, 2016, and to all my colleagues there, especially Tony Baker, Greg Garrett, and Dan Joslyn Siemiatkoski, who read and edited drafts of my proposal to Wipf and Stock. I am thankful for Gary Slater who reached out to me during his work on his dissertation, introduced me to his phrase "nested continua," and developed a scholarly friendship with me over a pipe of tobacco on my front porch. I am especially grateful to Steven Tomlinson and his amazing mentorship and consultation as an experienced scholar and teacher. His mind has an amazing gift at discerning patterns, and our conversations led to clarifications of my thought and insights into the most fitting forms of presenting my research.

I am grateful to my fellow members of the Liturgical Theology Seminar at the North American Academy of Liturgy, for their critical insights concerning my research and their encouragement for me to continue. I especially want to thank Gordon Lathrop for not only his scholarly mentorship, but also pastoral presence through my transition from constructive to liturgical theological scholarship. My heart is filled with gratitude for the many enriching conversations with and encouragement received from Louis Weil. I am grateful for Walt Knowles' amazing liturgical knowledge and willingness to talk things through with me. I am grateful for Joris Geldhof's friendship, scholarly dialogue, and encouragement to present my research at the LEST IX conference. I am thankful for my friendship with Matthew Olver and his amazing grasp of theology and extensive liturgical knowledge.

Thank you, Christine Havens. I am thankful to have had you as a student and I am grateful for your work as a freelance writer, editor, and formatter. I could not have completed the manuscript of this book without your constant commitment to its completion. I have had amazing research assistants throughout this period of my research. Thank you to Scott Painter; I am grateful for your patience. Thank you to Travis Smith and your enthusiasm for this research area. Thank you that after your graduation and ordination we have been able to develop an ongoing friendship. Thank you for your encouragement in this ministry. Thank you to Vivian Orndorff who kept me organized and helped model how to simply get things done. Thank you to Caleb Roberts. I am grateful for your brilliant mind and your uncanny bibliographic memory. Your dedication during the final push of the editing of this book has made it possible. Thanks to Joshua Woods for help with the index. I am especially grateful for Tarah van de Wiele. Tarah, you are brilliant, helpful, and I have never known anyone who could research with the ease of breathing. Thank you for your important work in setting up my initial research in this area and for our ongoing scholarly dialogue.

Thank you, Kelly, my wife, for all your patience and encouragement. This book is dedicated to my children, Vitaly and Maria. They will grow up and they will come to love and research the things that bring them life and joy. They may never read this book. It may forever remain the kind of thing in which they simply take no interest. And, if so, it will be meet and right. But the time they allowed me to "be at work," even though I was clearly sitting at my computer at home, the joy we took in one another when each "work day" finally came to its end, and my undying love for them are the fuel that brings this book, finally, to completion. Thank you, my loves.

Introduction

Liturgical Theology as Economic Anagogy

This book ventures to answer a set of questions about the nature of liturgical theology. To what does a theologian truly refer when uttering the word *liturgy?*[1] What is a properly *theological*, and not simply historical or anthropological, referent for that word? And, for that matter, what is the central meaning or task indicated by the word *theology*? And how might these mutually define one another? Each chapter answers these questions in a way appropriate to a particular definition of theology and liturgy under examination, generating meaning through the mutual interaction of these definitions. The conclusion then synthesizes these contemplations with the cumulative result of a kind of Christian realism, an apocalyptic realism.

In order to establish a solid foundation for the rest of the chapters to follow, this introduction presents liturgical theology as economic anagogy, where liturgy is taken as an example of human economic behavior and theology is defined as anagogy, a particular kind of analogical discourse. I first describe theology as anagogy. Then I look at an economic understanding of the nature of liturgy where I situate liturgy within its historical matrix. Next, I provide a preliminary approach to liturgical theology where the economic context of liturgy provides an analogy for the divine economy. I then note recent worries about liturgical theology in general and especially the approach represented by the phrase *theologia prima*. Finally, I provide an outline of the chapters to follow.

---

1. Aidan Kavanagh contributes to liturgical theology the phrase *theologia prima* and the approach to theology it warrants. With that phrase in mind, further questions along this line include: In what sense is liturgy *theologia prima*? And what does such a phrase tell us about liturgy on the one hand, and theology on the other?

1

THEOLOGY AS ANAGOGY

This book is situated within a stream of Christian tradition that emphasizes the transformative, contemplative, and ascetical nature of Christian theology.[2] The classical meaning of *theology*[3] is itself cultic. Theology finds the words appropriate to hymn the deities.[4] The earliest church avoided the word *theology* as it was a word coined within pagan philosophy.[5] Indeed, theology is just the highest form of pagan philosophical contemplation. One of the earliest uses of theology within the community of the faithful was to describe God's own inner life and our ability to contemplate it.[6] Denys would apply the word *theology* to Scripture, at least by implication, for he named its authors "mysterious theologians."[7] Over time, the word came to mean, by a kind of discursive extension, the "doctrine" of the Trinity, which is to say, the teaching of the Christian encounter with God in Christ.[8] Finally, by the late medieval period, theology began to extend to cover all sacred teaching, even those parts that would previously have been called the divine economy.[9]

2. See Evagrius Ponticus, *The Praktikos & Chapters on Prayer* where he clearly sums up and passes on this tradition. See also the works of Henri de Lubac, particularly *Medieval Exegesis*; *The Mystery of the Supernatural*; and *Corpus Mysticum*. Finally, see Aaron Canty, "Balancing Letter and Spirit."

3. See the now famous article by Frank Whaling, "The Development of the Word 'Theology.'"

4. In this sense there is no distinction between *theologia prima* and *secunda*. I am indebted to a conversation with Walter Knowles for this point.

5. Becker, *Fundamental Theology*, 64. See also Jenson, "Gratia non tollit." The old opposition between theology and philosophy is illusory. Philosophy was pagan theology. Plato et al. were theologians. The relationship between pagan and Christian theology is not easy as it cannot be mere rejection nor wholesale purchase. Grace sustains and perfects nature. Natural (that is to say, lacking in the revelation of the God of Scripture) theology has the potential to get many things right, but will never reach, on its own, the clarity of revelation. The relationship demands the discernment of spirits. Fortunately, we have a centuries-old tradition that has wrestled with these quandaries before our generation.

6. Evagrius Ponticus, *The Praktikos & Chapters on Prayer*, 15.

7. See Pseudo-Dionysius, *The Complete Works*, 152. See also Nicholas of Cusa, *Metaphysical Speculations, Volume 2*, for a reference to the biblical writers as "divine theologians."

8. See Gregory Nazianzus, *Theological Orations*.

9. So, for example, Aquinas's summary of *Sacra Doctrina* is called the *Summa Theologica*. Note, however, that we are not yet addressing the use of the word *theology* to denote general Christian scholarship, let alone the name of an academic field of research

For our preliminary definition, theology is that which searches for the [7] highest possible level of human *pattern recognition*. That highest level of pattern recognition includes transcendent, even divine, pattern recognition. Thus, unlike many immanent sciences of our day, the task of theology is not only to allow for, but to seek out transcendent causality, with the highest recognizable pattern being that of the Triune life of God and the Logos that makes God, even if suprarational, nevertheless intelligible.

Faith, like any form of human perception, is a noetic event wherein patterns are discerned—in this case transcendent, even divine patterns. Theology, like any form of human knowing, brings these perceptions into[1] intelligibility through contemplation. Take, for example, a stereogram as an analogy.[10] A stereogram generates an illusion of depth, allowing for the three-dimensional apprehension of an object on a two-dimensional field through a technique that allows for stereoscopic vision. At first the viewer sees only incoherent markings on a two-dimensional surface. With instruction, for example, as to how to hold the two-dimensional surface and what to look for, together with rules of thumb or "tricks" in order to instantiate a first apprehension, such as "cross your eyes," or "look beyond or through the page," a subject may eventually see the three-dimensional object emerge out of the otherwise incoherent subject matter. Immanent pattern recognition is like studying the incoherent markings one mark at a time, cataloguing them and determining their frequencies and ratios to one another. Faith is like accepting the techniques and even counter-intuitive advice and thus finally perceiving the pattern that transcends the two-dimensional surface.

The language of traditional Christian thought is one that not only allows for, but expects transcendent yet "non-competitive"[11] causality.[12]

under conditions of modernity.

10. See Johnson, *Knowledge by Ritual*, in which he explicitly links ritual to knowledge, where ritual behavior prepares the way for and enables a certain kind of knowing. An astronomer has gone through the ritual behavior of setting up, directing, and focusing a telescope to the point that the behavior has simply become a somatic extension for his or her own ability to apprehend the night sky. An astronomer has an encounter of the night sky that no non-astronomer will ever have—even if they happen to own a telescope. Our knowledge of much ancient and Old Testament ritual would be like one who had a telescope and a user's manual and then declared herself to be an astronomer! We have, in many cases, simply no idea what knowledge the ritual behavior of the temple granted the priests.

11. Tanner, *God and Creation*, 152.

12. Such an approach to theology is possible following de Lubac's retrieval of a non-competitive relationship between nature and grace, creation and divinity. That approach

God's being does not compete with that of God's creatures. Thus, there is no competition between immanent chains of causation and their ultimate transcendent, divine causation. Given the qualitative difference, however, between the infinite God and finite creation, divine pattern recognition is severely limited in both what it can confirm and in the relative depth of its explanatory accounts. Revelation is necessary for genuine knowledge of the transcendent.

Discourse about revelation, however, is not univocal, and therefore not literal. Rather, it demands *analogical* language as its most appropriate form. Analogy[13] compares two things based upon a correspondence between the two established in a recognizable set of proportions. Discursively, analogy often appears as a kind of metaphor. And although such theological language must remain strongly *metaphorical*, the realities under discussion are not *merely* metaphorical. The comparison, correspondence, and proportionality may indeed be quite real. That is to say, analogy is *ontological*, not merely linguistic or conceptual artifacts of human projection. Analogy is not imagined, or invented. It is discovered.

Now, if analogy is not an *artifact* of discourse (unlike many kinds of metaphor) but a discursive *discovery*, then analogical discourse is metaphor that discloses ontology. It is therefore apocalyptic in nature; it unveils something previously hidden; it grants familiarity without necessarily granting comprehension. Patterns pass through and manifest within varying media, like sound waves passing through water or, better, sound waves passing through the metal sheet of a sand table, shaping geometric patterns in the sand—generating differing yet analogous patterns along the way. The pattern is recognizable across the different media within which it manifests because the pattern transcends any given instance. The fact that patterns transcend any given manifestation, whether in terms of given instance or medium of manifestation, makes pattern recognition possible. Patterns manifest in media. The same pattern may be recognized across many different instances within many different media. This example helps us to remember how analogy is not merely discursive, but *ontic*. For the waves of sound in the air (pattern), transfer to analogous vibrations in the

---

continues with David Burrell, especially in *Creation and the God of Abraham.*

13. See Douglas, *Leviticus as Literature,* for the difference between analogical and dialogical thinking.

sand table (medium), creating still further analogous patterns in the sand (yet another medium).[14]

A wonderful thing about the use of analogy is that it allows for discourse about continuous realities.[15] Consider another example—that of analog as opposed to a digital recording. With analog recordings, the data is isomorphic[16] to the continuous flow of physical reality being recorded. So Ella Fitzgerald's voice is recorded onto a gramophone record in a manner just as continuous as that of its original medium, her voice itself.

A digital recording, on the other hand, divides her voice up into a finite series of slices defined by a finite amount of binary coding—imperceptible (supposedly) to the human ear. The worry about perception is due to the fact that the ear is an organic, and therefore analogical, organ. The rises and valleys deep within the groove of the record are homologous to the compressions in the air that allow human minds to hear Ella Fitzgerald sing. This ability to transfer the continuous and arithmetically infinite pattern from one medium to correspond proportionally to that of another medium is what makes analogical recording technology possible. Although not a literal, ontological infinitude (such as God), dynamic realities such as the human voice represent patterns that, when we attempt to map them arithmetically, force an impossible infinitude due to their continuous nature. After all, you cannot make a perfect arithmetic map of a geometrical relationship.[17] What makes analogical transfer possible within the realm of the sensible corresponds to what makes theology possible within reality as a whole.

Now this analogy between physical analogues and reality as a whole allows for all sorts of other wonderful theological fields of play. For example, the difference between digital and analog recording may form an

14. Notice that I use analogy in order to explain analogy. There is no other way. So here I ask the reader to notice the ubiquity of the analogical transfer of patterns across media throughout nature and accept its applicability to theology as given, at least for the purposes of this book.

15. Hoff, *Analogical Turn*, 60–75.

16. Isomorphic (or "equal form") is a mathematical term for two shapes that correspond to one another, yet allowing for inversion.

17. Hoff, *Analogical Turn*. For example, consider the arithmetical expression of the geometrical ratio of pi. Circumferences are not, in fact, infinite; the circle actually closes, even if, expressed arithmetically, the ratio of radius to circumference forces an infinite series of increasingly but never exhaustively accurate expression. Xeno's paradox is solved when we realize that walking from point (a) to point (b) is a geometrically and not arithmetically expressible activity.

excellent analogy for the difference between knowledge construed as representation as opposed to participation. Further, any time a pattern transfers from one media to another, there is noise. Noise is the random fluctuation, the entropy, the loss of energy to heat, to patternlessness, that occurs within a medium from the sheer impact of the energy necessary for the manifestation of the pattern itself. The goal of recording technology is to reduce the signal-to-noise ratio. This is the ratio that expresses the amount of energy that continues as the desired pattern compared to the energy dispersed as noise. Perhaps that is what we are doing when we pray: decreasing the signal-to-noise ratio in the transfer of the divine pattern into the media of our human lives. After the fall (or even simply due to the nature of our finitude) there is a direction of entropy as we move away from God, either in being or in perfection. The "noise" increases as we move away from the source of the "signal." The goal then, is return to the source.

One way to keep this analogy going in the direction of our return to our source could be to shift from an analogy to recording technology to another technology concerning the transfer of intelligible sounds, those of radio transmission and reception. A radio receiver must be tuned to the frequency of the carrier wave in order to receive and ultimately translate into sound the desired radio signal. Perhaps created persons are not unlike such receivers. We are designed to receive patterns and understand them. But in order to receive the signal and render it intelligible, we must be "tuned up." When the receiver is not only detuned, but perhaps even in a state of disrepair, tuning up to reality becomes impossible. The Christian life is that of tuning up to the eternal Logos, the ultimate transcendent pattern, and transferring it into the medium of a human life. Grace restores the receiver. The Spirit tunes and transmits the signal. We recognize the Logos in the lives of the saints.

We may also bring in all sorts of musical and sonic analogies. For example, resonance, the reinforcement of a signal due to the synchronous vibration of a neighboring object, allows the vibration of one object in space to set another object in harmonious vibration through any shared media, e.g., a piano will begin to hum if you open the dampers and simply wait long enough for the ambient sound to set resonance in motion. Is this perhaps not unlike the music of the spheres? The *sanctus* of the seraphim? Is this not like the sempiternal song that Christians hope to join in their earthly liturgical activity?

Finally, we may also make topographical and cartographical analogies, distinguishing cosmology as a rational, discursive account of the universe from cosmography, a kind of continuous physical modeling, an analogical map of the shape of the universe, e.g., for the ancient Near East, a temple, etc.

Analogy, as revelatory, founds, disciplines, and enriches the classic three ways of theology. These are the apophatic way, the cataphatic way, and anagogy. Now the apophatic is the *via negativa*, the way of denial whereby we contemplate God by naming what God is not. The apophatic way leads to knowledge of God by denying of God all that would be inappropriate to attribute to divinity: finitude, limitation, dependence, derivation, reduction, materiality, etc. All classical theology falls under what I will call the *apophatic imperative*. That is to say, no discourse concerning divinity can go against the rule denying direct attribution from creaturely language. A key problem with apophatic knowledge of God immediately presents itself. We cannot know God well following only this apophatic way, because to know what something is *not*, is not to know what it *is*. If you need to pick up someone at the airport and I describe only whom he or she does not resemble, you would be hard pressed to identify that person in a busy airport terminal. So the classical tradition moves to the cataphatic way, the way of affirmation.

The way of affirmation is still under the strictures of the apophatic imperative and may not suggest univocal contemplations, only analogical. Even when engaging in positive predication, those attributes are understood to be by analogy only, not simple identity. Nevertheless, the goal of the cataphatic or analogical way is to affirm what would be inappropriate to deny of God. It does so by attributing the superlative, super-abundant version of that attribute. So, for example, although we must deny materiality or corporeality to the divine nature, the following claim grates against a classical theology: God is not, or has no, mind. Now, strictly speaking, we encounter mentality, or noetic states primarily in their creaturely and finite manifestations. The classic tradition, nevertheless, would affirm that it is inappropriate to deny God mentality because it is more superior to have a mind than not. Thus we attribute mental status to God, but in the superlative: God is *omni*scient. Even positive attribution falls under the apophatic imperative, the apophatic stricture of theology. God does not have a mind like human beings or even, perhaps, angels. God has "mental states," analogically and superlative to any mental states we encounter within God's creation. God is omniscient, and omniscience does not simply name a quantitative distinction between God and creaturely mentality. It names a *qualitative* distinction. Whatever God has that is analogical to created minds, it is infinite and absolute—and thus, in many ways, simply impossible to conceive. We find ourselves, even in our positive attributions of divinity, in a certain sense in no better state than we were with our apophatic claims. In the case of the apophatic, we could not know God well, because to know what something is not, is not to know what it is. Here we cannot know God well because in the end our attributions are so superlative as to be incomprehensible to a finite mind. What now?

The third and highest way of divine attribution forms a kind of reversal of analogy: anagogy. In anagogy, God, or God's mighty deeds, become the primary thing predicated, with all creaturely predications realized as mere analogues to this fundamental divine meaning. For example, we do not know God to be love on analogy to creaturely loves. We know creaturely loves on analogy to God. Now we are speaking anagogically. Each of the three ways provides nested boundaries to each subsequent way. Both subsequent ways are subject to the apophatic imperative defined by the fundamental *via negativa*. And anagogy itself remains a type of, and nested within, analogy. But anagogy becomes an analogy that is reversed, where God, the divine nature itself, becomes the key term from which analogy is built and the creaturely becomes the analogue to God. Thus, the apophatic imperative is obeyed: direct attribution of God is denied by continuing, as with regular analogy, to recognize the incomprehensibility of any divine attribution. And yet an end run is performed around some of the epistemological problems derived from both the purely apophatic denial and the merely superlative analogy. With God as the primary referent, we are ensured a kind of contemplative, yet nevertheless direct, knowledge of God when we recognize the creaturely analogues as apropos via participation in the divine attribute itself. Thus, faithful knowledge of the creature "lifts us up" (*ana-gogue*) to its true and divine source.

Denys is a primary exemplar of the classic three-ways. In his *Divine Names*,[18] Denys first builds up a radically apophatic denial of any finite analogies from creation for divine attributes before reversing the analogy: that which is denied about God becomes affirmed when God is suddenly understood to be the actual and only proper referent of any given name,

---

18. See Pseudo-Dionysius, *The Complete Works*. See also the present author's work, *Theology as Ascetic Act*.

with creation itself now forming the analogue to God. In this book, instead of single predicate names or attributes I use liturgy, the cosmic liturgy as a whole, as an analogue for the divine economy, and eventually even the divine life itself.

Anagogy itself allows us to see that the various human activities, subject matters, and disciplines that we call *theology* actually name only one thing.[19] Theology can be seen and discussed under three main facets: God in God's very nature, the capacity for and gift of contemplation, and the sacred Scriptures and their faithful interpretation into the lives of saints. These three are nested within one another. These loosely correspond, delightfully but unsurprisingly, with the persons of the Trinity itself. God the Father is God in God's own nature, God the Spirit grants the gift of contemplation of God, while God the Son is the Logos, the Word of God, perfect reflection of the Father, given to us for our contemplation in the Holy Scriptures. These are, of course, one. The Scriptures provide the material for the Christian contemplation of God. Contemplation names the human capacity to know God at all. By classical definition, the God who can be known is, in God's own nature, a life of contemplation. True theology is nothing less than a share in God's own self-contemplation—to the degree possible and at the appropriate analogical remove.[20] That is to say, human contemplation is not equivalent with or identical to God's own self-contemplation. But insofar as it is a genuine contemplation of the divine it is a human manifestation of, and share in, the divine contemplation.

The three things we may properly call theology, the divine nature itself, contemplation of the divine nature, and the Holy Scriptures, are thus one anagogically. In anagogy, the higher reality becomes the defining term,

19. I follow Henri de Lubac's retrieval of the pre-modern theological unity of exegesis, contemplation, and Trinity (or the doctrine thereof, or, better, the rule of faith). *Contemplation* names the verb of theology, its doing. *Holy Scripture* names the substance of theology, the material contemplated. See Wood, *Spiritual Exegesis.*

20. See Hart, *The Experience of God,* which helps us define the content of contemplation. Hart is ecumenical and even inter-faith in his approach, boldly claiming that all monotheistic religions share the same or at least broadly compatible natural theologies of God, including not only the Abrahamic faiths of Christianity, Judaism, and Islam, but also the various Indian sub-continental philosophical religions, such as some of the more philosophical forms of Hinduism, Sikhism, Jainism, and, he believes, certain theistic forms of Buddhism. Hart describes that in all these traditions the key to beginning the contemplation of God comes in the contrast between contingent and necessary being. The next step in our contemplation comes to us in the contrast between conscious and nonconscious being(s). Finally the very possibility of bliss signifies the presence of the holy and provides the third and final key contrast in our development of contemplation.

with the lower realities representing mere analogues of the fundamental and transcendent term. Thus, Holy Scripture is the written analogue to the human capacity for contemplation itself, and a chief and authoritative example thereto. Human contemplation is an analogue to the contemplative nature of divinity itself, and any true human contemplation is a share in God's own self-contemplation. Thus, the three realities we call theology nest within one another and manifest one another.

LITURGY AS ECONOMICS

Having explored theology as anagogy, we now turn our attention to the economic nature of liturgy. Economy is, among other things, a means by which human beings provide for and protect themselves, and, when possible, thrive. A barter economy exchanges goods for goods, in kind, and of equivalent value (at least ideally). The modern West is most familiar with a market economy. A market economy takes a barter economy to another level of abstraction, using money as an arbiter of exchange. Because a market economy is an abstraction of a barter economy, I will only compare and contrast gift economies to market economies. I will now explore gift economics in a bit more depth in order to link liturgy to economics.

Some areas of human life thrive under conditions of barter and market economies, while others prosper under a gift economy.[21] Things that do well under one economy may actually be hindered or impaired under the conditions of another economy. Dealing safely with strangers and maximizing alienable material objects works best under market economies. But such things as religious life, spiritual health, public service, pure science, and the arts all thrive under a gift economy. The previous list of spiritual and cultural goods and services cannot be articulated in terms of market

21. The following reflections upon gift-cycle economics depends upon and summarizes the work of Lewis Hyde, *The Gift*. In *The Gift*, Hyde argues from anthropological, ethnographic, and folkloric studies that certain spheres of life are better governed by different kinds of economies. Hyde is building upon a solid philosophical and anthropological tradition of gift economic studies, e.g., Marcel Mauss, Raymond Firth, and Claude Lévi-Strauss. Hyde's goal is to show that art is a gift and that art thrives best under a gift economy—thus granting an account of why art and the artist seem underappreciated and unsupported in the modern West's market economy. I am interested in Hyde's account because his summary of the gift economy as a cycle of gift-giving provides an insightful anthropological model for understanding the economic meaning of the various levels of household in ancient Israel.

value. They must have institutions of gift-exchange if they are to be supported by a given people.[22]

In order to define gift, we need first define *property*. Property is the expression of the will in things, that is to say, in things external to the immediate human body, so, the plowing of a field as opposed to a walk through the countryside. Property is the right of action in things beyond recognized boundaries of the human body. The field is "proper" to the farmer in a way that some unknown countryside is not to the afternoon walker. And in plowing the field, the farmer appropriates the field to his person in a way that the afternoon walker does not appropriate the countryside. Economies distribute property to individuals. Many cultures have all three of the main types of economy: gift, barter, market.[23] But any given culture may balance them with respect to one another differently, and they may define one in terms of the other in differing patterns. It is not that one is right and another wrong, it is about finding the right economy for the good or property that needs exchange.[24]

While markets exchange commodities, gift economies cycle gifts. Commodity has value, gift has worth. You cannot put a monetary value on a gift if it is to remain a gift. Exchange nullifies the gift. Value, on the other hand, is just exactly determined by its exchange with something else. "One man's gift must not be another man's capital."[25] Keeping a gift for growth and capital, even if the gift is from a greater to a lesser party, is a violation of the gift. It ceases to be a gift and turns into a commodity.

Now a gift-exchange between two would produce mere reciprocity. A true gift-cycle requires three or more. A gift-cycle goes beyond mere reciprocity. When a third party enters, the gift increases. In circular exchange, no one immediately receives a gift from the same person to whom they

---

22. Each kind of economy is capable of supporting human thriving around appropriate areas of human existence. But each is also capable of misuse leading to human suffering. Hyde admits straightforwardly that gift economies can also be used to oppress, bully, manipulate, and justify. He presents the work of Millard Schumaker and Garret Hardin ("The Tragedy of the Commons") to balance his more positive reading of gift-exchange. He admits that he is trying to make a point about what is good about a fairly used gift economy in the face of the modern dominance of the market. With this regard my goals overlap with Hyde's.

23. A market may name a further level of artificial abstraction within the more organic barter economy.

24. That said, in a Christian theology, where all is gift from God, it is hard to imagine placing any other economy in explanatory priority.

25. Hyde, *The Gift*, 4.

give a gift. At least not of the same type or kind. The circularity of the gift-exchange does two things. First, it avoids D. H. Lawrence's *egoism a deux*.[26] This *egoism a deux* is the kind of narcissism that ensues in relationships of two persons who are merely self-obsessed through their reflection in the other. We need a third (or more), mediating party or else the gift may descend into mere barter.

An example of a cycle of three is that of the Maori of New Zealand. The spirit of the forest gives food through surrendering wild game to the hunters. The successful hunters give a portion of the game to a priest. The priest burns a portion of the offering in a sacred fire that returns the gift to the spirit of the forest. The cycle is complete and the spirit of the forest may be expected to remain generous. We find an analogous cycle in the ancient Near East (ANE), ancient Israel being no exception, where the increase of the year harvested by the people of the land results in their offering of firstfruits to the priests, the priests finally offering a portion of the firstfruits to the god(s) of the people. Thus, the cycle is complete and grants an expectation of continued increase.

Next, and in part because of the above, a gift economy creates a shared ego, a shared body. Just as blood is not owned by any given cell, tissue, or system within the body, but rather, belongs to the entire body, so too the property exchanged in a gift economy is not, ultimately, owned by any of the individual members of that corporate body, but by the body as a whole. Again, as blood feeds and nourishes the life of the body, so too gift-exchange is exactly the circulatory system of a corporate human body—granting it life and nourishment. Common property yields a common life and discerns a common good.

Gift-exchange makes corporate human bodies possible: "perfect gift is like the blood pumped through its vessels by the heart."[27] Just as the circulatory system keeps the corporal body alive, distributing by the blood life-giving nutriment to each constituent cell, so too a gift economy keeps a corporate body alive, vital, thriving, by distributing life-giving material possession, extension, property, to each constituent member. And just as the blood is owned by the whole body, and not by any individual cell, so too the goods of a gift economy are not individually owned by corporal bodies, but are the property of the body corporate as a whole.

26. Lawrence, *Aaron's Rod*, 115.
27. Hyde, *The Gift*, 180.

Hyde reminds us of the Native Americans of the West Coast and their famous potlatch as a key example of the above. The potlatch is a goodwill ceremony that entails "Destroying our Wealth." It is a passing on from one generation to the next the gift of the goodwill of the forefathers. A given chief usually only gave one great potlatch as a celebration of their ascending to power. The attendance of the tribe serves as a pledge of their continued gifts to the chief family, while the overwhelming distribution of gifts on the part of the chief seals the chief's authority, proving the chief to be a means by which the god(s) distribute their abundance to their people. So, again, there are three main parties involved: the tribe, the chief of the tribe and their various totems, the god(s) of the people. And this should not seem foreign to us as Christians. For it is just like Solomon. When Solomon completed his temple, he held a *leitourgas*, a public festival, feeding all of Israel fourteen days (1 Kgs 8).

When someone receives a significant gift, they throw an elaborate party and feed everyone. Status and generosity are always associated in traditional societies. The big man is not the one who has accumulated, hoarded, the most, but the one who can give away the most without flinching. This is much like the Suzerain Covenant relationship of the ANE. There are even echoes in our own medieval Western past.

The mystery of the gift-cycle is that although at the level of the individual the gift moves and seems to disappear, be consumed, at the level of the whole corporate body the gift increases through motion. Although not necessary for every gift economy, nevertheless, and as opposed to market economies defined by reciprocity, a gift economy is open to transcendence, to mystery, to the god(s), and, ultimately to the living God. So the passage of property into mystery refreshes and keeps the corporate body alive and abundant. For the individual, gift economies feel like motion, but at the level of any given corporate body, the gift-cycle is simply homeostasis at least, and growth and thriving at best.

So, returning to our definition of gift, above, gifts cannot cross two independent spheres, gifts cannot violate the boundaries of a body. When a gift does so, it either ceases to be a gift and becomes a commodity, or, if it remains a gift, then the boundary is abolished and a new body emerges or a new member is incorporated into an existing body. Commodities, on the other hand, do the opposite. Commodities create a boundary where none existed before, e.g., selling basic necessities to a friend. A commodity is alienable, detachable from the owner thereof. A gift is an extension of the owner. While in possession, the gift extends its steward.

This brief sketch of gift-cycle economics may seem rather foreign because modern economic theory starts from scarcity and concludes with competition. Gift economics starts from surplus and concludes with motion. The gift must remain in motion or the increase, the surplus becomes spoiled, tainted, drained of its spiritual energy and thus lost. Gifts must stay in motion for property in stasis turns stagnant, bloated, and corrupted. From the point of view where gift economy is assumed and market economy is explained rather in its terms, then market exchange exists for a secure economy between strangers. Scarcity comes only when the flow of gift-giving is stopped up.

But it is not just motion that maintains the gift; it is also its total consumption. If you want to keep surplus and abundance, you must utterly consume it. The best way to consume it is to pass it on. Under conditions of a gift economy, a gift is property that perishes. The gift must utterly perish for the giver. Note such perishing is different from the market-economy's consumption. Understanding this kind of consummation of the gift is difficult for modern Western folks, but it has not completely ceased to exist. The practice carries on in the church potluck, the family dinner, the gag gift passed on from year to year at the family Christmas, etc.

Before you can give a gift away, you must become equal to the gift. Between reception of and passing on of the gift the recipient suffers gratitude.[28] Passing on the gift is an act of gratitude. But if we cannot become equal to the gift, if we cannot pass on a gift equal to the gift received we must somehow perform an act of gratitude. Gratitude requires an unpaid, and perhaps un-payable, debt. Sometimes we are faced with an inability utterly to consume the gift, e.g., when the gift is spiritual, infinite, or both. An abiding sense of gratitude motivates labor in service of the gift. When the gift cannot be consumed, it must be passed on through action. For example, the artist cannot utterly consummate her talent, so, out of grati-

---

28. See Leithart, *Gratitude*. In the main I benefit from and find myself in agreement with most of Leithart's work. In this case I must differ. Leithart asserts that circulated gifts are not genuine gifts because they demand the debt of gratitude and eventual return in kind. But God's gifts are unconditional. Leithart's vision is a bit too Protestant for me. It seems to be an example of grace overturning, rather than sustaining and perfecting nature. Grace and mutual exchange are not that contrary to one another (see Stephen H. Webb's review of Peter Leithart's *Gratitude* in *Christian Century*, April 2014). In fact, in a model of satisfactory atonement, grace enables and sustains mutuality.

tude, she adds works of art to the world and teaches others how to harness similar talents found within themselves. Gratitude names another way in which the demand to keep goods in motion sustains property as gift—even in cases where the return can never equal that received.

At this point, we have begun to engage the vertical dimension of gift-exchange. Gift-exchange is precisely the best form of economy for those goods that are not, ultimately, the property of any human individual and that most clearly come as gifts from some reality that transcends the mundane, human realm. Furthermore, at the core of any working gift economy, there must be some founding gift, some fundamental donation that sets the cycle in motion. There must therefore be a primary giver. That donation, in ancient Greek language and culture, was called *liturgy*.

Leitourgia was the ancient Greek name of the Greco-Roman civic gift economy common throughout the Mediterranean basin.[29] *Leitourgia* was any act of public service by a private citizen at her own expense for the public fiscal obligations of members of the ruling class to her fellow citizens with regards, especially, to the funding of education, choruses, and the necessary public feasts (sacrifices) that always accompanies such donations. All this functioned within an ancient gift economy. Patronage functioned as part of an economic system that depended heavily on specifically signified exchanges involving social debt—and indebtedness.[30] The deliberate, potlatch-like destruction of wealth in turn aided the populace, the benefaction allowing and sustaining their own, peer-level gift-cycles.

At a merely anthropological level, liturgy is a ritual[31] action that connects (or attempts to connect, or claims to connect) with transcendent Reality or realities through analogous behavior. As its most frequent referent, the word *liturgy* refers to a human ritual behavior. The translators of the Septuagint did not choose the word *liturgy* by accident in order to describe the activities of the Jerusalem temple cult. Christians adopted the word

29. See Homan, *The Hungry are Dying*.

30. Thus, according to Holman's analysis, the early Christian emphasis on alms and other acts of charity to the poor as fundamental Christian divine service.

31. Defining ritual is beyond the scope of this project. Kim Belcher's definition from an anthropological perspective should suffice. Ritual is a system of mutually-interpreting human behaviors that serve as connective tissues between a culture and the inculturated bodies that exist within this culture. Notice the need for metaphor drawn from the corporal body to make sense of the body corporate. I am thankful to Matthew Olver for passing on Belcher's definition from a lecture he heard at The University of Notre Dame.

liturgy[32] because it represented an *economic* gift[33] on the part of a wealthy patron giving money, goods, or beasts for a notable act of public service. This gift involved sacrifice and festival.

Scarcity and competition form the ubiquitous ground of economic, and, in many ways, metaphysical, theories under conditions of modernity. But there is another economy we can intuit as human beings: a gift economy. Gift economics provide a key to unlocking truths about God's mighty deeds, God's relationship with creation, even the divine nature itself. God is a gift to God's self in the life of the Holy Trinity. Human beings, the cosmos as a whole (angels inclusive), are invited to, and included within, that flow of gift. In God we "live and move and have our being" (Acts 17:28). Our very existence as creatures is a donation of being from God on our behalf. We, in turn, return this gift in "living sacrifice" (Rom 12:1–5). Jesus is the third and mediating party in this exchange, our priest forever, "after the order of Melchizedek" (Heb 7:17; Ps 110:4). The fall has congested this divine gift economy. As a result, we fear our overtures to God will be rejected. Jesus has done the work to reconnect us with the Father.

Such discourse demands answers to certain questions. What is our means of participation in this divine economy? What is our (proper) role? And how do we play it out? How do we respond to God's fundamental, grounding gift? What is left for us after the flow is stopped, we have fallen from grace, and the direction of scarcity and entropy becomes our unavoidable course? How has Jesus restarted the cycle of exchange, the flow of the gift? How is he our fundamental re-founding donation? Each of the following chapters in this book builds to answer these questions.

ANALOGY AND REALITY

In this book, I will assume that reality itself consists of a series of analogically-related "nested continua."[34] Analogy is the way in which patterns translate across media on a given scale and up and down levels of scale

---

32. There has been some recent criticism of the old etymology of *liturgy* as "work of the people." See Aune, "Liturgy and Theology." Such critique does not significantly alter, but only helps the task of liturgical theology. Rather than "work of the people," "public service on behalf of the people."

33. Ibid.

34. A phrase adopted from Slater, *C. S. Pierce.* See Diagram A, in the appendix.

across differing nested continua.[35] In order to understand how I am using "pattern," and "media" here, consider the example of iron filings within a magnetic field.[36] We do not see the magnetic field, or sense it with any of our human senses. We discern the presence of the field because the iron filings follow its contour lines, filling up the space with the form demanded by the field. The pattern is the magnetic field—whether sensible or not. The iron filings are the media in which we are currently able to sense the pattern.

Now a magnetic field and iron filings, technically, exist on the same (empirically definable) plane. Thus, they share the same continuum, that between energy and matter. That continuum itself is nested within the time-space continuum. Now apply this empirical philosophical account analogically to God's created cosmos and God's relation thereto. Christians who believe in a providential Creator-God who is Logos, and therefore self-consistent, should not be surprised at such analogues.

Now what do I mean by *nested*? What I mean is that each level of reality can be concrete, isolable, and possessed of its own divinely granted integrity while nevertheless participating in patterns shared across these continua and, in fact, taking part in their transmission. Thus, Christians understand themselves to have direct access to the Father through Jesus Christ, and yet the tradition affirms that the angels continue to possess a mediating role, both directions. Interestingly, the non-competitive relationship that God enjoys with his creation finds its echo in grace-filled relationships across levels of creaturely reality. That is to say, in a state of grace, higher continua do not compete with lower continua. So, for example, the angelic worship does not trump human worship—it sustains, mediates, and shares in it. The one nests within the other.

These manifesting patterns are dynamic, patterning realities, not static objects. A dynamic account of what is going on around us as human beings gives us a proper ordering to our own, nested human continua. The various continua and media of being human form and inform dynamic, not

35. I borrow this language from the architect Christopher Alexander in his theory of design as a language of recursive patterns up and down differing levels of scale and across different media. He is particularly noted for his unconventional theory of design and his *Pattern Language* has gone on to be influential in the realm of computer science. There, it provides a means of designing computer languages and applications that retain a kind of flexible, almost organic freedom. See Alexander, *Notes on the Synthesis of Form*, *The Timeless Way of Building*, *A Pattern Language*, and *Nature of Order*.

36. Alexander, *Synthesis of Form*, 15–27.

static realties. A simple logical sketch of those dynamics is as follows: First, persons have an encounter with something other than themselves. Second, said encounter results in a behavior. Third, a concomitant discourse may follow.

Encounter precedes behavior; behavior follows encounter. Behavior precedes discourse; discourse follows behavior. And all of the above cases do so both logically and ontologically. Unfortunately, after the fall, we also use discourse for justification and rationalization. We use discourse to justify behavior we have already chosen. We develop a logos for it. Here the old geometrical maxim from grade school comes in handy: not all rectangles are squares, but all squares are rectangles. All discourse is behavior, but not all behavior is discursive. All behavior forms an event, but not all events are (human) behavior.[37] The geometrical relationship between squares and rectangles provides a useful analogy for the relationship of discourse to behavior, and behavior to encounter.

Let us now turn to our encounter with being human, for much of what it takes to understand the nature of liturgy is a sound Christian anthropology.[38] Sound Christian anthropology includes a psychosomatic unity of body and soul. The body is our media for being human; it is the media of our soul's expression. Human being is inherently embodied. Furthermore, our embodiment is not purely individual. Peter Brown shows how the body of the individual can enact that of its society or that of an alternative society in the face of the more dominant society.[39] We encounter our human embodiment, as the media of our existence, manifesting along a continuum from the corporal to the corporate body. And the corporal is not the same as the individual as constructed in a secular, "excarnate" "social imaginary."[40] This correlation discovered by Brown in his scholarship is not

37. The anthropology and theory of language represented by these definitions and metaphors conforms more or less closely to that of Charles Taylor in *The Language Animal*, and of course, the tradition he engages before, i.e., Gadamer. See Diagram B, in the appendix.

38. Secular anthropological insights are amazingly helpful, but may also mislead as they will normalize the normal and name abnormal the expected, after the fall. This is one of the central corollaries of de Lubac's insight into the problems that ensue when we move from a one-end to a two-end anthropology.

39. See Brown, *Body and Society*.

40. See Taylor, *A Secular Age*. Taylor's "social imaginary" gives us a better sense of the reality of human corporate embodiment. But the connotation of the word *imaginary* worries me. Taylor does not intend its negative connotations and is no mere constructivist. But I will avoid the term as it may be taken to connote that society is a kind of mass

arbitrary, but ontological. Bodies always implicate other bodies: corporate to corporal, corporal to corporate, etc. I call this the *somatic continuum* of human embodiment. Phenomenologically speaking, we never experience ourselves purely upon one pole of our embodiment.[41] We always find ourselves somewhere along the continuum of corporal to corporate.

Of course, secular psychology can only imagine such a "hive" as a "fictive kinship."[42] But if the corporate describes something ontological, then, regardless of whether or not one can devise an empirical test, the social organism is in no way fictive in nature, but real. The hive imagination is as real as that of any individual human being. The hive and its mind, as a sense of transcendence, are distinguishable, but nevertheless relatable and real.

Although Adam, as a whole, may indicate the entirety of humanity, over time, as one vast corporate body, there is not just one corporate human body. Just as various continua of the cosmos may nest in one another, and just as corporal bodies may overlap and interpenetrate through various forms of intercourse, so too do corporate bodies overlap, moving in and out and through one another, interpenetrating one another through various forms of concourse. Concourse names the benefits of economic relationship among persons within a corporate body, and various corporate bodies with one another. Economy is not only inherent to, but, in some ways, constitutive of our corporate embodiment as human beings. Liturgy, also, is a behavior inherent to our corporate embodiment. And liturgy is an economy.

Human nature nests within the cosmos and crosses the continua of heaven and earth as an incarnate soul. Thus, we could find a pattern not only crossing media, but also manifesting up and down levels of scale, always apropos to the media in which it manifests. Ascending up cascading continua, we move from the human, somatic continuum, up through that of the psychosomatic continuum of the unity of rational soul and its somatic expression. From there, we continue through the cosmic continuum that expresses heaven through earth. The cosmic continuum in turn nests

---

fiction of nevertheless actually completely individual and individuated human beings. Many modern, secular societies may well be fictive or merely imaginary.

41. See Diagram C, in the appendix.

42. See Haidt, *Righteous Mind*, for his summary of the "hive switch" in psychological research; this gives an interdisciplinary cross-validation. I only use this language of "hive mind" following Haidt's discussion of the same. My continuing point will be that what Haidt as a modern psychologist calls "hive mind," corresponds to pre-modern encounters with the human reality of corporate bodies.

in the continuum of infinite to finite being that characterizes the relationship of God to creation. Finally, all these continua nest within the divine continuum enjoyed by the fellowship of the Father, the Son, and the Holy Spirit.

Some qualifying notes before moving on to the next section: the above terms and definitions form key components to a functionalist-style Christian anthropology of performative embodiment. This functional approach provides a more sound anthropology than either an immanent essentialism or a social constructivism. The shared pattern of our humanity cannot be reduced to an immanent, static ideal or to an exhaustive account. That is to say, the pattern cannot be reduced to its manifestation at any particular level of scale nor to any one media in which we find it. Nevertheless, there are limits on possible sound instances of what it means to be human—some constructions distort rather than manifest the transcendent pattern. Because of this approach to anthropology, I am comfortable, together with the post-critics, making ad hoc use of anthropology and anthropologically-informed historiography because it is more critical or at least relativizing of the modern myth of the secular than sociology, psychology, and historiography thusly informed.[43]

LITURGICAL THEOLOGY AS ECONOMIC ANAGOGY

This anagogical vision of nested continua is a gift to liturgical theology, because liturgical theology is the discourse that corresponds most closely to ritual as behavioral analogy. If we assume, as Christians, that our liturgy not only claims to connect us with God, but also actually does so, then the ritual of the liturgy is not arbitrary, but is rather an organic analogue of reality. In an analogous cosmos of nested continua, the liturgy provides a field for anagogy. But if ritual—liturgy—is behavioral analogy, to what is it analogous?

Patterns express themselves in media and they both exceed and precede the media in which they manifest. Human economic behavior forms a key, if not the key component to our corporate embodiment. Liturgy is a human medium in which we discern an economic pattern. This pattern is not an immanent pattern, but a transcendent one: the divine economy. Any

---

43. See, for example, a contemporary social psychologist such as Jonathan Haidt and his plea for more anthropology to correct Western psychology and its modern, secular assumptions. See also Taylor, "Two Accounts of Modernity."

human behavior named liturgy, if it is liturgy, translates, participates, manifests, and gives, *in nuce*, this one divine economy. Liturgy is a medium in which we discern theology, transcendent patterns. Liturgy is an economy, an inherent medium of our embodiment. Anagogy is the highest form of theological pattern recognition. Liturgical theology may thus perform an anagogy upon economic behavior. Just as with the stereogram, once you learn to see the three-dimensional image in the previously incoherent markings, it becomes nearly impossible to return to your previous benign ignorance.

Liturgical behavior of the ancient Mediterranean required a founding donor. God is, of course, the founding donor of the cosmic economy. The earliest economic contexts of this word, *liturgy*, is a boon to liturgical theology, for God the Father offers the sacrifice of his Son on the altar of the earth as the "public service" that benefits the city of God.[44] We encounter a non-competitive transcendent God. Our behavior in response is our own liturgy, a ritual analogue to the divine gift. The analogy is reversed and we discover ritual itself to be anagogy. Our corresponding discourse becomes the discovery of anagogy, the reversal of the analogy for our human contemplation: liturgical theology as contemplation of the ritual anagogy. This chain of nested analogical continua makes liturgical theology possible and helpful. But not all liturgies are divine service. Our human world is riddled with false gods and idols. What do we do about such entropy, such noise in the "signal"? I take up and address this question in Chapter Two.

Ancient Christian theology clearly distinguished theology proper (defined in its threefold nature, above) from divine economics. The divine economy is God's mighty deeds, his way of relating to that which is not God, his "keeping house." Anagogy names a way of making divine attributions, a way of talking about God. In this book I propose to extend anagogy to divine economics. There is risk, of course, in any anagogy. There is significant risk in extending anagogy from something so clearly complicated and human as economics—especially while remaining clearly within the bounds of the apophatic imperative. So let me make myself clear and qualify my intentions. The goal is to apply to divine economics the same technique as that of anagogy in divine theology. That is to say, the goal is to locate creaturely analogues to God's mighty deeds and then name these descriptions as most appropriate to the mighty deeds of God—the human

---

44. This will be a major focus of Chapters Three and Four. Of course, the Son also offers himself freely, in union with the Father. See Anderson, "Sacrificial Offerings."

actions forming only manifestations thereof at an analogical remove. A central argument of this book, therefore, is that liturgy is a central focal point for such economic anagogy.

But I will not stop there. Sometimes I will also push the economic anagogy back into the very divine life of the Trinity. Any economic claim about God must ultimately be fitting to the divine nature. So, although economy and theology must clearly be distinguished, doctrinally, and practically speaking, nevertheless because the economy must be compatible with the divine nature we must therefore assume it to be, in the end, a manifestation of God that reveals the divine nature to us. Ultimately, therefore, the divine life of our Triune God must name an economy, a liturgy, if liturgical theology is to provide foundation to any truly coherent Christian theology.

Taking Denys's divine names as starting point, I approach liturgical theology as a kind of economic anagogy. In other words, I will not only take Denys's names of God as indications of anagogical attributes, but I will also take the liturgy itself not as something to be denied (apophatic) in order to understand God's mighty deeds, nor even as merely helpful metaphors (verbal or conceptual analogy) for which modern thought could grant us better vocabulary and conception; rather, I will take liturgy[45] itself as providing an economic anagogy into the best and most mystical language for the divine economy. Anagogy presumes ontological analogy from the transcendent to the immanent, from God as primary referent to creatures, or even creation as a whole, as analogical extension.

Throughout this book, I will take an economic approach to liturgy, but I use it to empower analogies for the divine life and God's mighty deeds, the divine economy. I then reverse that analogy in order to achieve anagogy. In each chapter, I will say how the liturgy is theology, at its deepest, trinitarian level. Thus we will be able to nest our human discourse about liturgy into the deepest possible continuum of theological contemplation. This nesting of the medium of liturgy into the pattern of a trinitarian economy performs an approach to *theologia prima* and allays recent scholarly worries.

45. Before we can define human liturgy, we must define liturgy theologically. That is one goal of this book. On the human, concrete side of liturgical reality, by *liturgy* I certainly mean any concrete human performance thereof, inclusive of the Christian divine service and then, by relationship and derivation, many of the other rites of the church. With regard to questions concerning *which* Eucharistic liturgy or tradition and *which* church, I must say that such definition is beyond the scope of this book, but that the goal is to provide a kind of criteria by which we could judge such issues. Assume a broad, lowercase *c* catholicism with regard to such questions at this point. I am grateful for conversation with Matthew Olver, who encouraged me to be clear on this issue.

SOME WORRIES

Schmemann inaugurated liturgical theology[46] with the work of liturgical renewal in general and the respective work of Dom Gregory Dix and Henri de Lubac in particular.[47] Dix's and de Lubac's retrievals overlap and implicate one another. Indeed, Dix's emphasis on the shape of the liturgy and its rediscovery of the ordo, combined with de Lubac's *corpus verum*, provided the elements from which Schmemann would synthesize liturgical theology. If liturgy makes the church (de Lubac) and the liturgy has its own internal dialogic (Dix), then that internal dialogue is the church's fundamental theology (Schmemann). Recent criticism has called into question both the roots of, and synthesis that is, liturgical theology.

Liturgical theology as an academic discipline is only about a half a century old at the publication of this book. In that short time, it has often defined itself over against other disciplines and approaches to liturgy, e.g., purely historical studies of liturgy, ritual theory, school theology, and the like.[48] Schmemann's liturgical theology entailed the rejection of "scholastic theology,"[49] his own pejorative phrase for Westernizing tendencies in Eastern theological scholarship.[50] Our problem as Western Christians is that we have so believed *lex orandi lex credendi* that, having "renewed" our liturgies, we believe we have already done the work of renewing theology. I submit that this work is not yet done.[51]

---

46. See Schmemann, *Liturgical Theology*, but, more importantly, the way in which the task and goal of liturgical theology is both performed and achieved in *The Eucharist* and *For the Life of the World*.

47. Recent scholars have named a "Schmemann-line" of liturgical theology in which different scholars include different theologians. See Aune, "Current State," 48.

48. Schmemann's *Liturgical Theology*, among other things, works out what liturgical theology is as opposed to the dominance of historiography in the field of liturgical studies. Fagerberg's seminal work has a similar goal. I am grateful to Gordon Lathrop who reminded me of Dwight Vogel's generous definition of liturgical theology in *Primary Sources of Liturgical Theology*.

49. See Schmemann, *The Eucharist*.

50. See Pott, *Byzantine Liturgical Reform*. Liturgical renewal in the East is, as of now, almost entirely theological. Their liturgies need renewal, but there is no mechanism or mutually recognizable authority by which this work could be done. It may be safe to say that Schmemann and his liturgical theology *are* liturgical renewal in the East.

51. A brief note about listening to the East: the Eastern approach to theology or liturgy is not, qua Eastern, superior in and of itself. I do not promote exoticism. Two things must be said to clarify this issue: Schmemann is almost as radical in the East as in the West. He is a controversial figure. Our listening to him as Western theologians and scholars

Kavanagh, in an attempt to follow Schmemann before him, asserts that the task of liturgical theology is to elucidate the way in which the liturgy itself is the primary instance of that which the word *theology* denotes, what he calls *theologia prima*:[52] "doing liturgical theology comes closer to doing *theologia prima* than *theologia secunda* or a 'theology of the liturgy'[;] . . . doing primary theology places a whole set of requirements on the theologian which are not quite the same as those placed on a theologian who does only secondary theology."[53] Further, a "liturgical act *is* a theological act of the most all-encompassing, integral, and foundational kind."[54] This basic assumption has recently come under fire:[55] in a truly Christian theology, no merely this-worldly *human* practice could serve as its primary instance. God is incarnate, yes, so theology proper must be and in fact is this-worldly and human in one important sense. But, according to such criticisms, the incarnation is *Jesus Christ,* not a repeatable and infinitely variable human activity.

Related to the above issues around *theologia prima*, I find three major concerns in the literature critical of liturgical theology.[56] One concern is that liturgical theologians reflect upon liturgy in a way that abstracts the ritual mysteries from their concretion in history and as human expressions.[57] In other words, the worry is that liturgical theology is too abstract, too generalizing, and not *liturgical* enough, where the word *liturgy* names a human, concrete act. This line of criticism throws into doubt what seems to be too romantic a view of liturgy found in the shape approach inherited from Dix.

A similar criticism, one that comes from the point of view that historiography provides a superior approach to liturgics, questions the

---

is not a "listening to the East," per se, but listening to one of her theologians. Secondly, insofar as Schmemann does represent the East, the East is worthy of our attention at least in the interest of ecumenism and rectifying centuries of Western parochialism, and, more importantly, because the East in general, and Schmemann in particular, represent a theological tradition unaffected by the Western semantic shift of *corpus mysticum* and *corpus verum*. Lubac has shown us how this shift has been disastrous for us in the West.

52. This is the primary goal behind Kavanagh's phrase *theologia prima* in *On Liturgical Theology*.

53. Kavanagh, *On Liturgical Theology*, 75.

54. Ibid., 89.

55. Aune, "Current State," 48.

56. Aune, "Liturgy and Theology," 61–65.

57. This is a kind of ritual theory approach.

chronological validity of the notion that liturgy represents *theologia prima*. Issues concerning the catchphrase *lex orandi lex credendi* fall under this category as well.[58] There are clear cases in history where theological arguments and reasonings *chronologically* precede liturgical formulations, verbiage, and activities. Both of these worries are characterized by an immanent and historicizing construal of liturgy. The first historicizes liturgy (another form of immanentizing) by asserting that the fact that, chronologically speaking, discourse has shaped liturgical behavior in the human past trumps any anthropological or ontological notion of the priority of behavior over discourse. The second immanentizes liturgy by making its truest form only concrete and punctiliar instances, with no two ritual instances ever alike.

Another concern is that liturgical theologians have reduced the liturgy too much to an expression of a given community rather than as an act of God on behalf of God's people. In other words, the worry is that liturgical theology is too immanentizing and not theological enough.[59] Such questioning calls into doubt how helpful a return of the church to *corpus verum* is for theology. If we make the church the true body, do we not reduce God to an expression of local community?

Another question deriving from the concrete study of history concerns whether or not we should translate *liturgy* as "the work of the people." The worry is that such a translation furthers what is already an overemphasis on human community. Recent developments in our understanding of the original context of the word *liturgy*, as described above, where liturgy is an economic transaction, is a boon in helping to mitigate against this. Interestingly, these two worries are opposite to the previous two. These latter worries are that liturgical theology is not concerned with transcendence and grace nearly enough.

The solution usually granted to the first and final set of concerns is to turn to the concrete, the particular, and study it historically, and perhaps sociologically, or anthropologically. If there is any theology left over, then focus on the transcendent and avoid reduction to community, thus solving the second concern. If there is no theology left over, well, more is the pity

---

58. Aune, "Liturgy and Theology", 53, quoting Paul Bradshaw "when believers come to worship on a Sunday morning, they do not come with their minds a *tabula rasa*." See Bradshaw, "Difficulties in Doing Liturgical Theology," 191.

59. Again, Aune is the key and best expresser of this concern.

for so-called "liturgical theology," but much the better for the advancement of sound liturgical scholarship.[60]

Although I can understand each one of these worries, I do not agree with the solutions most recently proffered. The complete argument of this book concludes that these liturgical theological conundrums find resolution when placed within the ancient understanding of the cosmos as analogous, nested continua with the capacity to resonate with divine pattern together with an approach to theology as the anagogical unity of the divine nature, contemplation, and interpretation of Scripture.

THE SHAPE OF THE BOOK

Each chapter takes a particular definition of theology and a particular liturgical economy, at some level of scale, and combines the two in order to imagine liturgical theology. Chapter One takes theology as the Triune God and describes the liturgy as the cosmic economy of God—God's house. Liturgical theology is the house of God.

Chapter Two takes theology as the Incarnate Word and describes the liturgy as the sacrifice of Jesus, providing a liturgical soteriology. Jesus's incarnation and paschal mystery fittingly nests in the divine economy. Liturgical theology is the sacrifice of Jesus Christ. After these, the next two body chapters treat with what modern systems call "method" (Three) and "sources" (Four) of theology.

Chapter Three presents liturgical theology as the contemplation of mystery, where theology is taken to be contemplation and liturgy is described as a mystical initiation. The focus of this chapter is the way in which *anthropos* nests within the cosmos—and finds restoration to this continuum through the donation of Christ. The material contemplated is Holy Scripture, the subject of Chapter Four.

Chapter Four presents liturgical theology as figural interpretation of Scripture, where theology is biblical exegesis and mystical initiation allows and empowers figuration. Chapter Four includes a final exegetical reflection

---

60. Interestingly, we find repeated here, in current liturgical scholarship concerning the Christian mysteries, the same old pattern of liberal critical biblical scholarship: theologians get the leftovers of the Scriptures after an historicizing critique. If there is nothing left for theology, well then, more is the pity, but much the better for a sound liberal theology in a free world.

on the book of Hebrews in order to develop a figural interpretation of the sacrifice of Jesus Christ.

The Conclusion allows the book as a whole to show that economic anagogy leads to an *apocalyptic realism*. I will argue that, for liturgical theology to have any real traction as a discipline, and in order to keep it from falling into ritual theory on the one hand, or mere theological gloss on liturgical historiography on the other, liturgical theology needs to fit into the frame of a transcendent metaphysic that engages ritual as something that unveils higher realities. I call this apocalyptic realism.

Each chapter nests within the previous. God's own creation nests within the being of God, for "in him we live, and move, and have our being" (Acts 17:28). So too, the Son's incarnation within the cosmos, and his divine service therein, nest within this sacred cosmos. Thus, each concrete Christian ritual mystery is a manifestation of and share in this perennial and cosmic series of analogues. God is a life of self-giving contemplation— our own contemplation of God made possible only within God's own. Our contemplation nests within God's own self-contemplation. Our liturgical embodiment of that contemplation nests with the cosmic economy. The Scriptures are the collected authoritative contemplations of God within the church. Once we have a proper Christian "nesting" of these various levels of reality and media through which we flesh out our human existence, we may then begin to study concrete Christian liturgies. But that will have to wait for another work.

Chapter One

Liturgical Theology as the House of God

The household of God is liturgical theology, where liturgy is the economy of a shared household and theology is the invitation to share in the gift economy of the divine life of a Triune God. I first discuss theology as the (teaching of the) Trinity. I then define the kind of economy enacted in liturgy, that is to say, a gift-cycle economy, in order to give an account of the divine economy. From this account of God's house, I then spell out some of the implications of the liturgical nature of cosmos as an act of worship. God's house is the cosmos as both the dynamic of persons in relationship and as an artifact, or set of artifacts, that receive their shape from, and correspond to, these dynamic relationships.

THEOLOGY, THE TRIUNE GOD

Theology names the Triune God. For the Triune God is a God whose Son is Logos, the perfect reflection of the Father in the Spirit. God is the *Theos-Logos*, and, although super-rational, not irrational. According to the contemplative tradition, theology is the contemplation of God in God's nature and the nature of God revealed to us in Christ is that God is Father, Son, and Holy Spirit. The contemplation that God shares within his own life is the contemplation we may share in God's life. This means that, most properly speaking, it is God's own Triune life, not verbal or representational reflection about it or upon it, that is theology. The nature of God is to be a life of gift-exchange. The word *theology* also extends to those teachings and reflections that lift our mind to such contemplations.

Now the Triune life of God is a life of mutual indwelling, a divine economy, a perfect gift-cycle of love among the three persons. In this life of love, God creates finite persons who can share in this love, a divine economy. God creates a house wherein to dwell and to provide for his children. This household, this divine economy is the divine liturgy. This sense of the divine liturgy is a *theologia prima*. And, in an even deeper (or higher) sense, *theologia prima* is the very uncreated life of God—the mutual gift-exchange of the Father's substance among Father, Son, and Holy Spirit. God's economic behavior always accords with his nature and provides anagogical material for reflection. The Triune life of God may also be considered a gift economy, a liturgy. Thus we come as close as possible to the identity ⌐of liturgy with *theologia prima*. The liturgy that liturgical theology engages ⌐is not a local, historic human ritual, but the divine economy. The divine economy is an angelic liturgy that renders cosmos. A given concrete human liturgy thus becomes, for us, *theologia prima* only insofar as it is not merely a human action; but, through the gift of faith, God sweeps our action up into the divine economy: the house of God.

LITURGY AS AN ECONOMY OF GIFT

The philosophy of the Mediterranean basin at the time that God became incarnate understood ethics to be teleological, answering the question: how do we fulfill our inherent nature as human beings? And it acknowledged three levels of ethics: personal, household, and political. The personal corresponds to the corporal along the somatic continuum,[1] the political to the corporate, while the household falls somewhere in between. I assert that these are all one pattern of human teleology manifesting in their ways appropriate to their location along the somatic continuum. The modern distinction between politics and economics makes little sense here. At whatever level of scale we are trying to achieve human flourishing, we are talking about economics—how to provide and shelter human thriving, corporal and corporate. An economy and a house, or household, name the same thing: a corporate dynamic of mutual benefit and protection. At these differing levels of scale, then, we have different bodies holding different property—appropriate to their scale. As the expression of the will in things, property is the right of action in things, the right to use something outside

1. On the somatic continuum, see the "Analogy and Reality" section in the Introduction and Diagram C, in the appendix.

the boundaries of a given human body. Property may be rendered capital, or property may be given away as gift.

The economy of gift extends to procreation insofar as a human (corporate) body must procreate or cease to exist and thus fail to thrive. And this procreative extension is, in itself, liturgical in nature. Most cultures, and certainly Christianity, recognize human life as a gift. Thus we find the "giving away" of the bride; itself a corporate, tribal act. In many pre-modern cultures, and especially those represented in Scripture, the woman who is "given away" is no one individual's property. Her womb belongs to the tribe, to the race as a whole; her womb is the means by which humanity as a corporate body continues. It thus comprises a primordial gift, a donation.[2] On the other hand, the sacrifice of the firstfruits redeems God's right to the firstborn male.[3] So the womb cycles tribe to tribe, but the male-child, the seed, returns directly to God. Thus arises the necessity of a system of substitutes for the sacrifice of the male firstborn.[4]

The economy of gift also leaves behind a material culture in its wake. And, like all material culture, its accretions become part of the encountered environment over time. This material cultural accretion is liturgical as well. It is not so much that (ancient) cities had temples as (ancient) temples had cities. The material culture of a household, at whatever level of human corporate scale, will come to reflect the degree to which, and the means by which, that corporate body keeps the gifts that sustain it in flow.

Circulated gifts nourish human flourishing beyond the private and the individual. But gifts also connect us with the gods as well. Gifts commune with the group, with nature, the nation or people-group, and with their gods. Sacrifice turns the face of the god toward that god's people. Some compassionate gods, in turn, offer gifts to their people.[5] Hyde himself points out how this corresponds well to the description of sacrifice, especially that of the firstfruits, in the Jewish Scriptures and the Christian Old Testament.[6] I would add that both also correspond well to ANE temple cults in general.[7] A priestly order is set aside to receive the gifts of the people. Through them, the people offer gifts to (a) god(s). The god(s), in turn, return the gift with

---

2. Hyde, *The Gift*, 96–120.

3. Ibid.

4. Chapter 2 will elaborate on this system of substitutions.

5. Ibid.

6. Deut 26.

7. Pritchard, *Ancient Near East, Volume II*.

further increase. All human life is a gift. Hence, the covenantal demand of the firstfruits. Gifts in cyclical gift-exchange must be commensurate with one another, or, at least, returned through gratitude.

Hyde gives the example of Dionysus and the various corn gods of the ancient mystery cults. In these cases, the god (usually male, firstfruit) gives its life for others and then regains it at a higher plane. When honey rots, the spirit bubbles up within it—alcohol. Drinking the "spirit" passes the life of the god into the imbiber. The god of alcohol is broken into a higher life. So, in this special case, the god becomes incarnate and offers his own incarnate body as the gift that establishes the bond between god and human being. Sometimes, but not always, this gift heals a previous breach or separation.[8]

A primordial, founding donation makes a gift-cycle possible. Liturgy is concourse between higher and lower in gift-exchange. Liturgy is the gift of a benefactor, down economic levels, that enables sacrifice—gift-exchange in return to the beneficiary, up levels of economic status. This is true whether on the part of the wealthy benefactor to the population of the city-state on an earthly plane, or on that of the goddess of the city to her people on a transcendent plane. Thus, a liturgy constitutes a total gift-exchange among unequal partners that enables peer gift-exchange and grants beneficiaries a taste of peerage, even if through (divine) condescension. Donation commences the flow of the gift economy. This is liturgy, proper: a primary gift enabling sacrifice and gift-exchange; really, sacrifice as gift-exchange. Liturgy is simultaneously the founding act that sets the initial condition, and, because of that, the overall reality of gift-exchange across levels of wealth. Thus, liturgy enables sacrifice: literally, metaphorically, analogically and, following my main argument, anagogically.

When we take the anthropological description of gift economy as an analogy for the divine economy and then, anagogically, we reverse the analogy and place God's economy as its primary meaning, then God's gift economy becomes the originary and primary meaning of all economies. God gives the most primordial gift of all: a share in his own being. All anthropological insight flows out of reflection upon God's original household of creation and salvation.

---

8. Thus, the atoning capacity of sacrifice is secondary to and nested within its overall nature as a part of a life-giving gift-cycle.

GIFT ECONOMY AS HOUSEHOLD

Recall from the Introduction that *leitourgas* named a civic economic event that benefitted the city and her citizens. Liturgy was a gift-exchange from a wealthy benefactor at the highest economic level of human gift-giving. Liturgy was an essential part of keeping the gift in motion in the ancient gift economy of the Mediterranean basin. Liturgy was a dynamic economic activity. The very word *economy* comes to us from the Greek word for "house" or "household." For the ancients, an economy, a household, and a house were, if not one reality, certainly understood as echoes of the same pattern across levels of scale.

These levels of scale and differing media show themselves more plainly in the Hebrew cosmic project. Jon Levenson outlines three different meanings of the use of the Hebrew word for *house* in the Jewish Scriptures.[9] First, primarily, house is an economy that brings provision and protection, brings life, and brings safety from imminent death. We need to provide for our family and we thus generate those behaviors that build the provision and security of the household. Next, house means a continuing inheritance among the living for those who must die. House means (re-)generation. Part of the protection and provision of the household is insuring its continuance in the face of the inevitability of death.

Finally, house means a material culture that inherently follows these two previous core economic activities of provision and generation, behaviors that lead to the construction of more static "residue," manifesting in material culture a shape fitting to the dynamic of those very house-defining behaviors.[10] The shape of that material culture arises inherent to the activities it compliments. The result is the material cultural artifact or conglom-

9. See Levenson, *Death and Resurrection*.

10. See van de Wiele's "What Rights Get Wrong." She provides an excellent summary of recent biblical and archaeological work on the house in ancient Israel. The village, as opposed to rising urban settings in the later monarchies, was a *mishpachah*, a family or clan unit as a whole. These were part of a single *beyt av*, or "father's house." She notes how even the structure of the now-famous four-room house indicates a kind of egalitarianism across paternal heads of households, enabling them to be the "kinsman redeemer" not just for those literally within the father's house, but also for distant kin left as orphans and widows and then extending even to the land of the clan itself, daughters sold into slavery and even the avenging of blood "lost" to the *beyt av* through murder and the like. Urban conditions began to shift against this traditional folk culture and its capacity to solve such "social justice problems." Isaiah cries out against it when he says, "woe to you who join houses to houses" (Isa 5:8). In other words, the LORD will curse those who break down the egalitarian *beyt av* in order to increase a more individualistic system of wealth.

eration of artifacts we think of most directly and colloquially when we first hear the word *house* spoken in English, e.g., a house as drawn by a child. All of these different meanings of the Hebrew word for *house* are analogously resonant with each other in the biblical corpus and can each stand for the other.

Now let's look more closely at the activity itself, so that when we look at provision, procreation, and the residual artifacts, they will make more sense. A household of human beings needs to eat. In order to eat, they need to prepare food, often by cooking it. As human beings, they are communal, and thus they need to eat together for fellowship. After the fall (whether they are aware of the reason why or not), each individual member will suffer death. In order to maintain the perpetuity of the household over time, the household must have means of replicating itself and then providing protection and nourishment for its progeny. Thus, again, the importance of the practice of preparing, cooking, and eating food in such a way that includes those members who cannot feed themselves or yet engage in the preparation of food.

And so we find, over time, a kitchen: fireplace (or stove or oven), table, storage, and the like. The material culture gives only a glimpse of the entire dynamic in play—but when the dynamic at play is understood, each item and their respective arrangement with respect to each other makes sense: *kitchen*. This is true, of course, for many rooms within a given physical structure called a house and, at differing levels of scale, it is true for all levels of material culture that reflect and contribute to a shared corporate economy.[11] So, for example, the kitchen of a people group is her temple. The kitchen of a god is some allotted portion of earth, perhaps where her meteor has fallen from the sky. The kitchen of God is earth (hearth) as God's table.[12] House, therefore, names a dynamic reality of economy (provision and protection) and the securing of its perpetuity (progeny) that results in a (relatively) static reality, i.e., the object of material culture that the word *house* commonly denotes.

The three different meanings of *house* outlined above also provide material for anagogical meditation upon the divine economy. The economy of creation is a dynamic gift cycle—first within the Triune life, then granting

---

11. See King, *Private Dwelling,* and De Haan, *The Romance of Redemption: Studies in the Book of Ruth.*

12. Recall that in the temple the altar stood between the sea of bronze and the entrance to the holy place as earth falls between the sea and the visible heavens.

life to those invited to share. God ensures provision and safety for his children—the Sons of the Most High—even providing an heir for his throne: the Son of God. Finally, this dynamic activity of provision, safety, and progeny leaves behind and accumulates a material culture: the visible cosmos. Each of the following sections will expand upon these three in turn.

GOD'S HOUSE

The Divine Economy

God's being is the communion of Father, Son, and Spirit—a shared gift. The Father gives his own substance to his Son. The Father gives the Spirit through the Son. The Son in the Spirit in turn gives glory to the Father. The economy of the divine life is that of perfect circular gift-exchange. Notice that the gift-exchange of the Trinity is a perfect exchange, and not mere reciprocity—for there are three involved, not two. There is no *egoism a deux* in the Living God. The Father grants the Son and the Spirit a share in his own being without remainder. The Trinity is the perfect gift-cycle "shared ego." But this is anagogy. Any human gift-cycle manifests these analogies because it is a participation in and manifestation of the abundant life of the Triune God. God is the primary instance of gift-exchange. Our human economies are a finite analogue.

To create finite persons beyond the infinite persons of the Godhead is fitting to God's own superabundance and nature as a communion of gift-exchange. In the perfection of God's gift-exchange, the persons of the Trinity give the gift of being to finite persons. These finite persons, in turn, may share in the being of God, for "in him we live and move and have our being" (Acts 17:28). This divine donation performs the perfect liturgy: the donation on the part of the wealthy[13] benefactor that enables the well-being, or, in this case, any being whatsoever. Furthermore, the donation grants continued household, which is to say, provision for, and protection of, the beneficiaries. God's creation is therefore a great city, a heavenly kingdom, celebrating one great feast—its cosmos the holy order of its liturgical celebration.

---

13. Recalling that *ousios* in the Greek, as in English, can mean both "being," and "substance," as in "a man of substance," which is to say, wealth. The church fathers would pick up on this double entendre and apply it to the Parable of the Prodigal Son.

A gift usually works best between equals. Genuine gift-giving renders equal. Greater to lesser performs a service or benefaction, lifting up, even if only temporarily, the lesser. The Greeks called this *leitourgas*. The translators of the LXX adopted this word for the service of the tabernacle and the temple in Jerusalem. The early church continued its use into Eucharistic observance. Lesser to greater performs fealty or sacrifice—reaching out for the opportunity of mutuality across differences of power or scale. Sacrifice is gift-exchange across the inequality of heaven to earth. And when the sacrifice is true, and directed toward the living God, it attempts to cross the interval between the finite and the infinite. It is, therefore, dangerous.[14] It is no mistake that the second major pericope of Scripture involving a narrative of human beings is about sacrifice—and about its failure and the disastrous consequences thereto. For the invitation to enter into the mutuality of the cycle may be refused by the greater party who does not need it. And that is the risk we take when we sacrifice to the Most High God. But if God himself performs the *leitourgas*, then the grounding fundamental gift that enables sound exchange ensures the acceptance of the sacrifice. Sacrifice is response to and part of the cycle initiated in *leitourgas*.

When God accepts our gift, the gift returns as the increase. The service of God, the divine service, God's *leitourgia* on our behalf, makes possible our sacrifice, our return in gratitude to God. Because we are in gift-exchange, the divine service on our behalf and our gratitude in returning sacrifice are one. (Indeed, they become perfectly one in the incarnation and paschal mystery.) And God grants this because he created us for relationship with him. The divine condescension and the gift of our own elevation in the Spirit enable the mutuality that makes relationship with God possible across the interval of finite to infinite.

Liturgy is a gift from a superior that establishes a household, an economy. God's liturgy is the benefaction that enables and empowers our sacrifice of thanks and praise, so that it can be successful—worthy of reception, generative of relationship. Misconstruals of sacrifice are bound to arise when understood non-economically or in a framework of the modern Western economy of scarcity and competition. Sacrifice has been greatly misunderstood and even despised. This is due in no small part to the lack of conscious familiarity with gift economies on the one hand, and

---

14. See especially Halbertal's *On Sacrifice*. The discourse engaged in this chapter already provides a kind of re-contextualizing corrective to Girard or Burkhart. More will be developed with this regard in the next chapter.

the methodological or ideological bracketing of that (non-competitive) transcendence that is always necessary for complete Christian accounts of reality.

The Sons of the Most High, the Son of God

A house provides an economy of provision and safety. A shared meal is a kind of house, *in nuce*; it is the dynamic enactment of sustenance, consummation, and communion. And God has built a house to live in. Heaven and earth are full of God's glory. But he does not live in the house alone. He provides for a mighty household, the household of his children. God does not dwell in a house because the God of the philosophical attributes needs shelter and safety, but because a glorious abode is fitting to his nature and because his children, the Sons of the Most High, with whom he desires fellowship, need shelter and provision. At the highest level of mythology preserved in scriptural record, we have the Sons of God, the council of the 'elohim, e.g., the council of the gods in the Psalms or the book of Job, the seventy gods appointed to the nations (Deut 32:8), or the twenty-four elders before the Lamb who was slain (Rev 5). God cuts an everlasting covenant with the 'elohim. Insofar as the ANE assumed a pantheon of sons around the Most High God, we receive material to build trinitarian anagogy.

Even before the fall, God's house needs shelter from dissolution to the nothingness to which it would surely succumb without the constant sustenance of grace. This shelter is the firmament: God's primordial donation for immanent fellowship among finite persons and with the infinite persons of the Trinity. Thus, liturgy and sacrifice are primordial, pre-fallen goods—ends in their own right—without need for human violence in their accounting. God separates the watery chaos above and below, and places a firm roof to keep it that way. God breaks the head of Rahab of the deep (Ps 89:10) and provides food to those in the desert (Pss 89:10; 74:14; Isa 51:9). God's household shares a meal, the eschatological banquet, the final consummation.

The ANE father of the gods and the Most High God of the Levant found in our Christian Scriptures provide material for anagogical contemplation of the God and Father of our Lord Jesus Christ.[15] The core ANE myth is that the gods find themselves hungry and threatened by chaos. They cry out in powerlessness to their father, the Most High. He looks for a champion,

15. See Levenson, *Death and Resurrection*.

and a champion steps forth. Sometimes this champion is his beloved son (as far as we know, always in the case of the Levantine mythology). The beloved son slays the chaos monster, establishes an everlasting covenant, and arranges a clever means by which the sons of god will be fed. Human beings will harvest and provide for them sustaining nutriment from the earth and they, in turn, will protect the nation or people-group under their charge. We find this theme in Scripture, narratively, throughout the Psalms but rather explicitly in Deuteronomy 32. It is against the mismanagement of this divine counsel that the Most High cries out in Psalm 82.[16] This over-all mythos should be familiar to Christians, as it becomes incarnate in Jesus Christ and revealed in the ritual mysteries and the Gospels.[17]

That God provides food for the angels from the material order sur-vives well into Christianity, sublimating all previous pagan sacrifice.[18] There is even analogical echoing in the order of sustaining consumption. God provides minerals for the plants, plants for the animals, and animals for his sons, the gods. When we, as human beings, eat animals, we imitate the angels, and, ultimately, God.[19] The problem with eating animals is not the supposed violence of their slaughter, but our presumptuousness. They are the food of the gods. Perhaps the forbidden fruit of the Garden of Eden corresponds, mythically (among other things), to the presumptuousness of animal consumption outside of sacrificial service to the divine. Only when we are elevated to our liturgical *imitatio Dei* may we partake of the food of the gods. Thus, Israel becomes God's children. In imitation of the 'elohim, they become the 'elohim of YHWH (even of the Most High God) and, espe-cially in the persons of the prophets, joining divine counsel with him.

That the Christian eschaton is also called the final consummation is no coincidence. God consumes creation. The heavens (that is to say, the angels) consume the earth (that is to say, in sacrifice). The paradox of such consummation is that, although "you are what you eat," certainly, also, metabolization of food entails a transformation of something into

16. See Coogan, *Stories from Ancient Canaan*. Furthermore, one can consider An-selm's interesting theory of angelic replacement on the part of the baptized in this light, as he is very close to the ANE myth. Christianity is a kind of divine "'elohim-replacement project." See 1 Cor 6:3–4.

17. See Lewis, "Myth Became Fact."

18. See especially the angelology of Evagrius Ponticus as found in his *Kephalaia Gnostika*. This sublimation is rather explicit in the works of Origen, implicit in that of Denys.

19. See Klawans, *Purity, Sacrifice*.

the creature that consumes it. The prey becomes the lion. The lower entity is, counter to entropy, integrated into a higher pattern and hypostasis. It requires breaking, eating, and digesting.[20] Thus, God solves the problem of entropy through consummation. God dines with his creatures and lifts them up. The final consummation is the theosis, the deification of the created cosmos. The consummation of earth by heaven is the perfect union of the sensible with the intelligible, for Christ joins all things together in himself (Col 1:20).

Even to call the Holy One of Israel "God" is to engage in theological analogy. For the word *god* is borrowed from previous pagan polytheism. The gods name the powers of this cosmos. The Holy One of Israel infinitely exceeds the name *god*. And yet it is appropriate as material for anagogy. For, we may reverse the analogy and note that the created powers are mere created analogues of their Holy and Infinite Source. ANE and the Levantine cosmology, at the time of the formation of the old covenant Scriptures, recognized an analogical relationship between a nation's god, a nation's king, and the father of a household. The Most High God was the father of the gods. The king was the father of the nation. An earthly father was a kind of household king. And these correspond to differing levels of economic provision and flow: cosmic, people-group, and local-group.

Liturgy renders a house. The divine liturgy is God's house. We find anagogical material for reflection at each level of scale: human father, human king, even ANE god or gods. We should find divine, even trinitarian analogy to an ancient pantheon no less surprising than our more familiar analogy of a human father and son. We need not be surprised or afraid when we discover that ancient Israel had much in common with their neighbors throughout the Mediterranean basin. It is the living God and his relationship to them, love of them, and continued manifestation to them, that makes Israel unique.[21] At each of these anagogical levels God provides, protects, and insures perpetuity through an heir.

20. Thus divine service involves martyrdom—the consumption of the corporeal for the sake of the Spirit. I will discuss the role of *martyria* in the economy further in the next chapter.

21. That the common beliefs of an ancient Israelite might prove to be simply an example of ANE and Levantine "polytheism," and not an exception, may be a frightening prospect to some. We do not need an historical, anthropological, or otherwise nominalist or abstract theoretical justification of the uniqueness of Israel. This is indeed dangerous to do, for either Jews or Christians, as it sets us up for renewed anti-Semitism. Rather, the uniqueness of Israel is an article of faith revealed theologically: Israel is unique because God chose them, and for no other reason. We come to know that God chooses Israel,

We may now move from house as provision, to house as progeny. God's house provides an heir for the continuation of the household. God does not need an heir for our fallen reasons; God is immortal, of course. God has an heir because God is love. The God of the philosophers needs no heir. Nevertheless, through the revelation of the Christian God in Jesus Christ, we discern that the Father indeed has an heir, "who was descended from David according to the flesh and was declared to be the Son of God in power according to the Spirit of holiness by his resurrection from the dead" (Rom 1:3–4). The revelation of God in Christ does not reject the ancient encounter with transcendence embodied in the myths recorded in Scripture, but it does change our interpretation of them.

At the next level of provision of an heir, we have Israel as a people and, concomitantly, we have the monarchical line of David, their anointed king. These share the same pattern, but manifest at different places along the somatic continuum. In both of these cases, we find God's providential concern with the death and resurrection of the beloved Son of the covenant line.[22] In the case of David, God provides an heir for the continued support and existence of the visible Son of God on earth, Israel, for "out of Egypt have I called my son" (Hos 11:1).

The doctrine of the Trinity is the sublimation of Levantine polytheism.[23] From the point of view of a more developed Christian theology, polytheism errs in two areas: The first concerns the familiar Creator-creation distinction. The second is less familiar, and concerns the divide between the infinitude of the divine persons and the, to us, transcendent but still finite persons of the cosmic liturgy, which is to say, the angels. Christian monotheism, revealed monotheism, agrees with ancient philosophical monotheism with regard to there being only one reality on the "god side"

---

not through immanent chains of causal reasoning, but by revelation. Because there is no anthropological, biological, or esoteric reason for their uniqueness, genocide cannot take any kind of foothold.

22. Levenson: *Death and Resurrection.*

23. See Behr, *The Way to Nicaea*, which provides a correction to some NT scholarship over historical theology and makes a case for continuity between the canon and the continuing early church in the oddly innovative conservatism of the development of trinitarian teaching. Here I am pushing the historical theology of our "doctrine of the Trinity" even more deeply than Behr, suggesting that the fully developed Christian tradition represents the final sublimation of Levantine polytheism due to the revelation of the living God, not in spite of, but, catholically, *through* that very culture.

of the Creator-creature divide. But, in the end, orthodoxy rejected a simple monism. "God is one, but he is not alone."[24]

There is only one divine reality. But is there only one divine person? The church's answer, of course, is that there are three. In other words, the previous gods of the Levantine pantheon did not all fall under redefinition as created angels. Some became recognized as uncreated persons of their own: the Son and the Spirit who proceed from the Father. Three powers, 'elohim, gods, became recognized as having been epiphanies of the three infinite persons of the Trinity. The rest the church came to realize were merely created finite persons, the angels.[25] Thus, the ontological divide of philosophical theology remains utterly intact with regard to divine and created nature. But there are three infinite persons on the divine side, and a multitude of possible finite persons on the other.

The city of God, the kingdom of heaven, reverses the analogy of the ANE city-state and household of the king.[26] The incarnation of the Son of God provides another recursion of the theme: the uncreated heir of God, Israel as God's firstborn, and David's heir as Israel's king merge into one, with the call to establish a divine economy, a new covenant, and build a new temple—a temple of his own body, corporate and corporal. Thus, the ANE totemic relationship of god, king, and people simply collapses and paradoxically merges into one: the Son of God becomes the human king of God's people; God's people become the corporate body of God's human Son.

The house of either a god or a human king is a mighty palace and a glorious economy with courtly practices. The court of the king on earth performs an analogue to the heavenly court of the god. The temple on earth of a given god performs a ritual homology to the court of that god in the heavens. A priest is someone set aside to perform the earthly homologue to the heavenly servants, courtiers, or angels. A prophet is a human being

---

24. See Hilary of Poitiers, *Sacred Writings*.

25. I am presenting this as a kind of historical theology, insofar as this anagogy was something that unfolded over time for the people of God. However, I am in no way intending this to form some kind of a mere "history of ideas," on the one hand, or a material genealogy on the other. I am engaging in anagogy with ANE mythology. I do so because I discern that is what the Scriptures themselves do. Insofar as I am aware that this is anagogy, under the strictures of both the apophatic imperative and the humility of analogy, then I am engaged in a post-critical retrieval and neither a univocal or equivocal reduction.

26. See Mumford, "What is a City?"

who has been invited behind the veil, no longer in ritual homology, nor in ruling analogy, but in actual encounter, in traditional anagogy or, even later, mystical experience.[27]

The divine *leitourgia* also establishes, within God's being, the household of finite persons. That is to say, the divine donation sets in motion the dynamic reality that is the heavens, the invisible part of the cosmos, the angels. Within this economy of abundance, finite persons in turn offer their sacrifices of fellowship to the only infinite persons: Father, Son, and Holy Spirit. And that liturgy is cosmos, holy order, bringing life out of chaos. The tradition teaches that the rest of creation joins this liturgy, hymning with it as it echoes down levels of scale, "unto ages of ages," and crosses through many media, "heaven and earth are full of your glory," before any human person ever engages it. But human beings, when elevated to our role and duty as cosmic-priests, share as created finite persons with the angels in this liturgy that renders cosmos out of chaos. It is, in fact, over this liturgy that Christ the high priest presides, and in him, Christians find their priesthood.[28]

That there is a totemic relationship between God, king, and the corporate body of Israel, that there is a shared pattern across these levels of scale and differing media, is not the problem addressed by revealed religion. The above represents a kind of organic human state, whether or not modern liberal ideology grants us the capacity to imagine it. Indeed, the problem is not even the abuse of this order by human beings—at least not primarily. The problem is the incompetence and maleficence of the angelic rule. God's solution is to become God and king for every nation and people, first, through Israel, then from Israel, to all nations where Israel—God's firstborn, will be a light to the world. God's incarnation as Jesus becomes the radically surprising way in which God makes good on this plan. The gods of the nations become subordinated as the angels. They are no longer anyone's gods. They are just messengers. The angels themselves are then judged by their new replacements—the *anointlings*, the little Christs, the Christians (1 Cor 6:3). Any explanation that assumes reductive accounts

---

27. See Hedley, *Living Forms*. Instead of worrying about empirical reduction, what if mystical experience is just what every prophet had? What if our access as Christians to mystical experience was the way in which Joel's prophecy is fulfilled in the new covenant? The prophet enters the heavenly court, sees God and his council and overhears their counsel. Some prophets are even invited to that council, such as, for example, Abraham. I will take this up again in subsequent chapters.

28. This insight will be the focus of the next chapter.

of myth, or conflates modern critique of myth with Christian apocalyptic condemnation of the gods does not help, but hinders understanding, and, indeed, Christian action. Liturgy under both old and new covenants is warfare. We worship the Lamb or we worship the beast.

Sensible Cosmos as Divine Material Culture

At the grandest scale, what is the material artifact that this dynamic activity shapes? Recall, liturgy names the initial gift that establishes an economy of fellowship across the gulf of unequal parties. Within, and because of, that divine liturgy, sacrifice names the dynamic activity that defines the relationship of created, finite persons within the life of the infinite persons of the Trinity—thanks and praise. This relationship between the dynamic economy and material culture of house grounds an economic anagogy for a fully Christian cosmology between Creator and creation, and also, down nested continua, between the "pure intelligences," or, angels, and the realm of the sensible.

House, as a dynamic reality with a corresponding material cultural artifact, manifests up and down levels of relative scale, human and divine: father (house), king (palace), god (temple). At each of these anagogical levels, the divine economy renders a material culture. The link between temple, house, and palace is that of the same pattern across differing levels of scale or across differing media. Liturgy renders a temple. The word we render "house," and "temple," are the same word in Hebrew and most ANE languages. Every temple is the house of the god and, in the case of the Most High God, forms an earthly homologue to the cosmos as a whole—God's true house.

Just as the Sons of God are the divine household, so, too, then the material culture of God and his household is the sensible universe. The house as a dynamic pattern of life and relationship among persons also forms, within the more relatively static—or, perhaps better, slower—dynamic reality around it, a material culture, which corresponds isomorphically with the same dynamic patterns. Within time, static realities really only name "static from our human time-frame." An oak tree is a dynamic reality. A mature oak may, however, appear relatively static over the course of a normal human lifetime. Another way to put it is that static vs. dynamic depends upon relative dimensional perspective. The more dimensions taken into account, the more static the instance will appear. The less dimensions, the more dynamic. So, for example, light seems to fling itself outward into space at an incredible speed. But modeled outside of time, where time represents a fourth dimension, we have a static object: the four-dimensional light cone, etc.

The physical reality arises in such a way as to incorporate the surrounding environment topologically while arranging a continuously growing material culture. That is to say, material culture becomes a kind of feedback loop within its initially formative dynamic. Thus, for example, liturgists are familiar with the old dictum, "the architecture always wins." This saying expresses the way in which no amount of liturgical modification can change the way in which the architecture of the church building itself will force a certain performance of the liturgy. Thus, a given material artifact feeds back into, and itself influences, the dynamic that initially formed it. For all church architecture expresses the prior dynamism of the divine service itself.

Thus, material residue accumulates and eventually becomes a part of not only the behavior, but even the encounter itself. The accumulating residue of material culture over time remains, nevertheless, homologous to the dynamics of the household in the above senses: provision, protection, and (pro-)creative maintenance. By economic anagogy, the cosmos itself opens up her mysteries as just such a household. Not only the heavens, but also the earth, are full of God's glory.

To sum up, I am proposing (at least) two major nested continua within God's creation: first, like iron filings in a magnetic field, cosmos arises when finite reality is poured into the dynamic relationship of the infinite and Triune God. This Christian cosmos consists of the heavens, who are created persons enjoying communion within a trinitarian "field." Second, and nested in the above, the sensible universe is like just such iron filings of matter,[29] in the angelic field of the cosmic divine service, forming nested spheres, descending down levels of scale within the created cosmos. "Heaven and earth are full of your glory": the dynamic of relationship among the pure intelligences in their cosmic act of worship both forms and uses the material cosmos as the pathways of their processions, the furniture of their actions (the philosopher's "furniture of the universe"), the gifts of their offerings—and all co-inhering within, and manifesting, the communion of the Holy Spirit. Again, like those iron filings in a magnetic

---

29. Whatever "matter" may be. Space precludes expanding on this ancient conundrum. See the works of Lloyd P. Gerson, especially *From Plato to Platonism*.

field, the material cosmos manifests as it does when the pure intelligences consume material, sweep it up into the field of cosmic liturgy. Thus, the cosmic liturgy forms the heavenly feast, the heavenly sacrifice.[30] Christian cosmology is angelology.

This vision of the relationship of the heavens to the earth does much theological work. We can see the extreme importance of the role of angels in creation, without making them creators or even co-creators with the Most High. We can name them the powers of the cosmos without the temptation to worship them.[31] We can also see, with eyes of empathy and compassion, the great human temptation to worship them, and the obvious, almost "natural" development of pagan religion due to the fall.

Another benefit of this vision is that we may retrieve the beauty and power of ancient Christian cosmology—even a Christian theology of pre- and non-Christian pagan myth—in such a way that shows us why, for example, the gods "need" sacrifice on the one hand, and why Ptolemy's model was so compelling for so many centuries on the other. And this insight into the relationship of heaven to earth gives us these payoffs in such a way as not to demand any given physical cosmography or "scientific paradigm," per se. Christian theology is thus empowered to makes sense of contemporary, quasi-empirical cosmography, without denying transcendence. We may retrieve a fully Christian cosmos, renewing the metaphysical depth of cosmology without canceling or disputing that of the kaleidoscope of popular empiricist cosmology. We can rejoice to give thanks to God for "galaxies, suns and planets and this fragile earth, our island home."[32]

Just as any quotidian household dynamic leaves behind and accumulates a more static residue (recall the kitchen example, above), so too the cosmos itself is the residue of a shared dynamic life, or, rather a set of nested shared lives: the Trinity, the 'elohim, human being. The relationship of the divine economy to metaphysics goes "all the way down"—for the God who transcends metaphysics grants a share in his own being in order to build

---

30. Consider Denys's "theurgical lights": the ancient theurgical defense of sacrifice is less conjecture and more descriptive in such a homological universe. See, for example, Platonius Sallustius' *On the Gods and the World*, where he argues that it is fitting to give to the gods in kind, as they have provided thusly. "Prayer without sacrifice," he explains, "is only words."

31. Think of Tolkien's "gods" (the Valar) in his *Silmarillion*. The Valar are the powers of Arda, the cosmos, who sing creation into being as a performance before the uncreated god, Ilúvatar. They express Ilúvatar's thoughts and are one with him.

32. *The Book of Common Prayer*, 370.

a house in which to dwell. And he does not dwell there alone, but with his entire household, the sons of the Most High. For "the LORD is in his Holy Temple, the Lord's throne is in heaven" (Ps 11:4).

CONCLUSION

Theology, proper, is the Trinity. The Trinity is itself an economy, a gift economy. This gift economy leaves behind a culture as its residue, a house as its artifact—the cosmos. Human liturgy is not a symbol of the divine economy; rather, it is its earthly and human analogue and means of participation and revelation. Returning to the issue of *theologia prima*, the divine life must be its most proper referent. This is the event we encounter as God's creatures in God's self-revelation. Any way we manifest or participate in the pattern of God's *theologia prima* becomes for us our *theologia prima*. And this is the essence of Kavanagh's insight. Liturgy is that behavior that provides us a medium in which to participate in the life of God (along with other important things such as, especially, *ascesis*). It is somatic in nature (so too, ascesis) and inherently embodied. Finally, theology is that discourse that corresponds (or ought to correspond) to and nests within that behavioral share in the life of the Living God. Theology is the discursive counterpart to our behavioral encounters with God.

What, then, is liturgical theology? Theology, in one key sense, is the Christian encounter with God as Trinity. Liturgy is a sacrificial household, a city-state economy, a cosmic temple that constitutes creation's grace-empowered response to our encounter with the living God. At a cosmic level, the liturgy of the angels gives matter back to God in a sacrifice of thanks and praise. The furniture of the cosmos is the result of the accumulation of artifacts, physical and intelligible, fitting to the shape of the activities of a cosmic liturgy. At the highest level of scale, liturgical theology is the infinite gift economy of the Triune God establishing the cosmos as God's house. Liturgical theology names the cosmos as God's own house in a dynamic sense that embraces a shared economy, a family lineage, and then an artifact of material culture, and thereby realizes the canonical context of the ANE temple as dynamic ritual analogies of God and the divine economy. By extension liturgical theology is also that discourse whereby we extend and contemplate the divine economy. A Christian cosmology places the earthly ministry of Jesus Christ within the mythos of Scripture's ANE temple-cosmos. In the next chapter, we will take up sacrifice as this divine gift-exchange extends to include substitution and atonement. Thus, the next chapter makes this general discourse about sacrifice, gift, and economy specific to Jesus Christ.

Chapter 2

Liturgical Theology as the
Sacrifice of Jesus Christ

As the previous chapter engages an economic cosmology, here we reengage sacrificial atonement as an economic act, and, therefore, as liturgical. Jesus' sacrifice in the visible realms nests within the economy of the cosmic, divine household as a whole. I first discuss theology as the incarnate Word. I then define liturgy as atoning sacrifice, through a brief look at old covenant sacrifice, in order to give an account of Jesus' sacrifice. From this account of Jesus' liturgy, I then spell out some of the implications for new covenant worship as itself sacrificial in nature.

THEOLOGY AS THE INCARNATE WORD

Theology is the Logos of God, the *Theos-Logos,* who is the Son of the Father, the second person of the Trinity. The Word of God is theology. Christianity is a deeply theologically-oriented religious tradition just exactly because it is the religion of the Word of God incarnate. The early Christians considered theology to refer to that part of the Christian gift of contemplation that related directly to God, opposing it to the contemplation of the created order, physics, which is to say, the economy.[1] Therefore, the God whom the Word reveals, and the internal life of communion enjoyed by the persons thereof, is also theology, proper. Theology, proper, is God's own Triune life and not merely verbal or representational reflection about it or upon it,

---

1. See Evagrius Ponticus, *The Praktikos* and *Chapters on Prayer.*

48

much less formulations or creedal accounts. All these are secondary, even tertiary.

In this sense, then, insofar as the divine service on earth is a human action, it is the ritual enactment of this *theologia prima.* Theology proper, for us as human beings in the realm of the sensible, is the incarnate Word of the Father, Jesus Christ. A given concrete Christian liturgy becomes *theologia prima* only insofar as it is *not merely* human action but, through faith (and faithfulness), God sweeps up and manifests within that human action theology proper: the liturgy of Jesus Christ. What, then, is the liturgy over which Jesus, our high priest, presides?

SCARCITY AND THE FALL

Before we answer the above question, let us return to our economic model as our definition of liturgy and our anagogical context. Recall that the increase of gift-exchange is not the same thing as the profit of market exchange. While turning a profit through continued exchange the increase is lost. Remember, "one man's gift must not be another man's capital." In contrast, exhausting the gift by passing on surplus property, although there seems to be no profit for the individual, the body corporate enjoys the increase. That is to say, contrary to the focus on individual return in a market economy, passing on the gift distributes the increase to the body corporate.

Commodities move to turn a profit. In this case the property truly is used up, because the externality of the exchange assures that it will not again return to the flow, to the circulatory system of the body corporate. By externality, I mean that the exchange is external to the body. The benefits accrue to an individual and the flow within the body is stopped up at one location. But if gifts move to share the increase, then gifts flow. They move, like water, to the lowest place, along the path of least resistance. *I* become poor that *we* may all become rich. The gift flows to the member of the body that has been empty the longest. Hence the law of gift economics: conduct no business within the tribe, conduct business only without, beyond the tribe.

In the Law of Moses, the Lord forbids usury within the house of Israel, while allowing it with strangers (Deut 23). Usury is part of the separation, alienation, of the market economy of commodities. It insures that there will be return when the body is allowed to "bleed out" for the sake of the stranger. Hyde gives the hypothetical example of an Egyptian who asks an ancient

Israelite for a bushel of grain.[2] You cannot assume you will ever see that grain again. You cannot assume the stranger knows about how one bushel of grain in the spring turns into several more each fall. You cannot trust his laws and customs to be similar to your own. The group—Israel—may suffer loss of some of its circulated wealth if you simply give to this stranger—the body may bleed out. There is always risk beyond the boundaries of a body. So you negotiate a contract with terms of return on interest. You demand goats as collateral. You sign it on paper with witnesses. In this way, some risk for the body corporate is mitigated, but—and this is important—the Egyptian walks away with the bushel of grain he needed. Relationship occurred, but it was contractual and safe—no boundaries were crossed, no new body created, nor old body dissolved or violated.

Roman law eventually developed a division between *res* and *persona*, things and person, allowing the alienation of "property" from its owner. Thus, the division of *res* from *persona* created a division within the previously unified notion of "property"—a notion developed to serve as a way of identifying an object with a person. The contract as a legal binding document arises, historically, as a legal fiction to generate an artificial bond to take the place of the now lost organic bond of the gift-exchange. If gift-exchange generates a corporate body, then gift-exchange across inequality often manifests a covenant. Contract presumes a fictional legal equality of disparate bodies. Covenant recognizes inequality and bridges the gap to form a corporate body. Covenant recognizes property as an unalienable extension of the person. Thus, property and ritual and moral purity cannot be separated from one another. Finally, and key to the distinction between contract and covenant: contracts, as external fictions, only work when enforceable by coercion. Gift-cycles are destroyed by coercion.[3] The organic bonds generated through the cycle of gifts only work when there is no coercion.

Eventually the Roman legal contract would come to serve as the social imaginary of Western civilization—the so-called social contract. Modern social contract theory thus sits uneasily on a double conceit:[4] that the passions undo social life, rather than ground it, and that coercion alone preserves social life, rather than proving a symptom of its dissolution. When we take gift economy as the more foundational analogue, we may assume on

2. See Hyde, *The Gift*.
3. See van de Wiele, "What Rights Get Wrong."
4. See Hyde, *The Gift*.

the contrary "that it is not when a part of the self is inhibited and restrained, but when a part of the self is given away, that community appears." [5]

When a gift is hoarded it disappears, it curses. From the point of view of gift economics, scarcity appears only when flow is diminished. Moneyed, i.e., artificial, wealth produces scarcity in its wake, and then names scarcity as the founding "law" of its economic tyranny. Thus, discourse follows behavior—in this case modern economic theory (discourse) following the increasing power of the bourgeoisie (behavior)—and, as often as not after the fall, to justify and normalize. When we turn one man's gift into another man's capital, we nourish that part of our being that distinguishes, separates, and alienates us from one another. Gift and market economies thus balance between emphasizing whole over part or part over whole. They both have a role to play in human thriving. When the whole is emphasized, we may sense that we loose certain individual freedoms. When the part is emphasized, we loose the spirit of increase and communion, fellowship.

In the *Politics*, Aristotle explains that there are two economies: household management and retail trade. [6] The first is natural; the second is artificial and potentially unnatural, in an immoral sense. The worst of all means of gaining wealth is a misuse of retail trade: usury, the charging of interest. Although retail is an acceptable abstraction (especially, as we have seen above, in the case of exchange of goods between strangers), when money itself—an abstraction invented to ease exchange—is loaned on interest and made to yield an increase artificially analogous to the natural increase of say, cattle stock or grain crops, we have taken it beyond its abstracted usefulness and created an unnatural perversion. [7] We construct money in order to ease exchange through abstraction, not in order for it to become its own source of increase through interest. Usury converts what would otherwise be generosity into a market exchange. What would have been a donation, a gift, an act of charity, becomes a loan—a chance for the individual to profit. So instead of using up property through the giving of a gift, a lender earns a return on a loan. In contrast with this foundational aspect of capitalism, there is increase in a gift economy—but it does not belong to the individual owner or lender, but to the body corporate as a whole.

5. Ibid., 120.

6. See Book 1, Chapter 9 of Aristotle's *Politics*.

7. If the contrast between natural and unnatural brings up unhappy connotations of modern nominalistic natural law, replace those words with the now more popular "organic" vs. "synthetic" or "artificial" to get the right feel.

A given people-group shuns the exchange of commodities to the degree that it sees itself as one body. The exchange of gifts will be avoided to the degree that given people and people groups see themselves as different bodies. Gift creates association and obligation. Commodity generates alienation and "freedom."[8] Neither of these are inherently good or bad of themselves, of course. There are times when freedom from obligation is the best course of action. But at other times obligation is the means of generating and maintaining the body corporate. "When gift exchange achieves a convivial communion of spirits, there is no call for liberty; it is only when our attachments become moribund that we long to break them."[9] However, it is just exactly because gifts bind that gifts must sometimes be refused. This is why gifts given to a judge are not called gifts, but something pejorative—a bribe.

Although hard to grasp under conditions of late modernity, understanding the logic of Aristotle's (and the vast majority of the Christian tradition's) take on usury requires not so much a belief in corporate bodies—as though corporate bodies are the kind of thing that may turn out to be mere abstraction and thus have no real existence of their own—as it requires the phenomenological recognition that human being exists as corporate bodies. The successive waves of Western "reforms"[10] have effectively broken down our otherwise innate ability to recognize the corporate in our human embodiment.

The Greek word for interest is *tokos*, "offspring" (as in the *Theotokos*). An abstract convention cannot yield offspring—only natural life can bring forth new life (or in a Christian theological frame, only God's creation can burst forth in divine blessing). Thus, for Aristotle, one of our "noble pagans," the most natural and therefore best form of economy was the household economy—a gift economy. The law against usury is a law that demands the submersion of the self into the tribe, of the individual ego in the corporate ego, the corporal body into the corporate.

---

8. I place "freedom" in scare quotation marks because market freedom is the arbitrary freedom of modern liberal politics, not the Christian freedom of rational direction toward one's natural end.

9. Hyde, *The Gift*, 91.

10. See Taylor, *A Secular Age*, 774. Taylor posits the centrality of a "Reform Master Narrative" in Western civilization, for example: the Carolinian Reforms, the Cluniac Reforms, the Lateran Reforms, the Protestant and Roman Reformations, the Renaissance, the Enlightenment, etc.

The myth that sustains the social contract narrative—the noble savage who is fine on his own but horrible when forced to live with others—exactly contradicts biblical narrative, and both historical and anthropological evidence. The early modern construct of the "primitive," as with most constructs, shows us more about early modern perceptions of vast difference between Western and non-Western people-groups (whether contemporary or historic) than anything concrete about human origins. Hobbes knew no social passions, only individual. Hobbes assumed the hive-mind was a mere representational construct, rather than a real living body. But if we assume a myth of fundamental corporate harmony—and that due to a primordial and divine donation, a donation that founds and sets in motion a gift-cycle—then the story we tell about economy, liturgy, and sacrifice will necessarily change.

Capitalism and communism are both mythical constructs forming the economic correlation to the fundamental metaphysical myth of violence. They are thus no real opposing ideological systems as they both assume scarcity and competition. They only argue as to who is to have property rights over capital: is it the abstraction of the multi-national corporation or the abstraction of the contractual nation-state? In either case, property is alienated, persons are excluded, and no gift is exchanged. Capital is already the cessation of a gift economy. Thus, liberal philosophical and political thought (including liberal theology) is that of the bourgeois, explaining (or justifying) behavior after committing to it. Let me make clear here that my point is not about capitalism as some possible historical-cultural reality, per se. Here I am simply using the word *capitalism* to name any economy or justifying narrative of such that finds itself removed from gift-exchange—and therefore its primary donation, grace.

Now this earthly description of gift economy gives us an analogy for the relationship of the transcendent to the immanent, of the heavens to the earth. How did we fall from God's good, abundant, grace-filled gift economy into our current state? A better, or at least more answerable question, is what does it look like when we fall, what has happened? The fall stops the flow of gift-exchange. Fallen from grace, entropy begins to consume finite being. An ontological entropy expresses itself at a human scale, among other ways, as scarcity and competition. The fall is the move from abundance to scarcity due to hoarding and ingratitude.

When a gift is hoarded it disappears, it curses. Scarcity appears only when flow is diminished. Translated into anagogy, economies of scarcity are themselves analogical manifestations of the fall itself: the free flow of grace and sacrifice between Creator and creature stops under conditions of presumption and ingratitude. The flow stops up on the finite, created, and human side of the exchange. We become bloated with gift, stagnant, fetid: "for on the day you eat of it you shall surely die" (Gen 2:17). How can we enter back into the flow of gift-exchange after alienation? Surely the party responsible for the alienation must restart the flow, must atone for its breach. But if the increase has been exhausted through profiteering, how can the offending party fund such a sacrifice? Before we see how Jesus restarts the flow between God and cosmos, we need to tie up a few more loose ends.

SACRIFICE AND SECULAR ANTHROPOLOGY

In sacrifice, we receive the gift of a divine-human gift-exchange, a divine concourse. Recall that return is part of the flow of a gift economy. The flow is not just of equal to equal or peer to peer, but of greater to lesser and lesser to greater. The difference that crosses this interval of lesser to greater is a donation on the part of the greater to the lesser. The donation is the liturgy. Sacrifice, enabled by and within the scope of this donation, returns the gift on the part of the lesser to the greater.[11]

For many, sacrifice means substitutional slaughter for atonement. Sacrificial atonement, even substitution, is rather a kind of therapy after the fall, within an already existing and inherently good gift-cycle sacrificial order. In fact, it is just exactly that good and grace-filled gift-cycle that makes such atonement possible. The sacrifice of Jesus Christ is not an act of scarcity, but an action assuming a more primordial abundance. I must first take a brief detour into some of the fear of sacrifice in recent scholarship.

Recall that at a quotidian and merely anthropological level, liturgy is a ritual action that connects (or attempts to connect, or claims to connect) with transcendent Reality or realities. The shape that action takes, nearly universally through human history and especially in the West, is that of sacrifice. Liturgy involves sacrifice.[12] Sacrifice is an anthropological fact

11. This liturgical gift economy is the background economics, for example, to the ANE Suzerain covenant.

12. See Hedley, *Living Forms* and *Sacrifice Imagined*. Despite the pleas of skeptics and rationalists, religion still persists under conditions of modernity. For similar reasons, sacrifice generates heated opposition in the secular academy. How can the slaughter of animals "make holy" (*sacra facere*)? Hedley takes up both of these issues and their relationship in the two books cited above, respectively.

almost as ubiquitous as opposable thumbs and upright walking. Liturgy is sacrifice in the ancient pre-Christian West and this was no different for the people of God before the coming of Christ. The liturgy of the temple was a liturgy of sacrifice.

There is a long and venerable Enlightenment tradition of secular analysis of religion as the perdurance of the merely barbaric into more "civilized" times. And that is due to the Enlightenment foundation-narrative of primitive violence as opposed to primitive communion.[13] Post-Enlightenment anthropological theories of religion and sacrifice follow suit: violence is the foundation of society.[14] The sacred that is made through sacrifice (here construed as violence) is not a projection of a given society, rather, sacrifice, as violent, produces social structure. The sacred forms a cypher for social structure itself. Given the secular rejection of transcendence in taking account of things, the "sacred," under such a view, is not "God," or "gods," but violence, itself, as the source of the sacred and its concomitant social ordering.

Such insights are penetrating hermeneutically and even, perhaps, phenomenologically, especially with regard to our fallen condition and its negative ramification upon "natural"[15] human religion. But insofar as they are asserted as anthropological, they fail; for they serve more as a hermeneutic imposed upon anthropological interpretation from an ideology of violence and scarcity, rather than the result of sound ethnological analysis. Even as a hermeneutic, it is one that axiomatically rejects sacrifice as proper for Christian analogy or metaphor. Such rejection cannot prove helpful to a canonical, scriptural Christian theology, nor to one in which God is revealed to command sacrifice. Christianity must have a positive account of ritual and biblical sacrifice.

---

13. Here I assume John Milbank's groundbreaking analysis of post-Enlightenment reasoning in *Theology and Social Theory*.

14. Perhaps the most ingenious form of such critique comes from the work of René Girard whose views I sum up in the above paragraph. My description of Girard's points is based in part upon Douglas Hedley's illuminative analysis. See also Burkert, *Homo Necans*. His work is genius and avoids the dismissive reductionism of Girard, but still holds to a violent origin for sacrifice that continues to correspond to Enlightenment narratives of human origin.

15. I place "natural" in scare-quotations marks because I am using the word "natural" here in the realist sense of "having to do with one's nature," and the teleology implicit in that. I do not intend to indicate any concession to a *natura pura*.

One could, nevertheless, argue for continuity with ancient sacrifice in Christianity, rather than a radical break.[16] Allow me an analogy. Imagine that zoologists were compelled, or felt compelled, systematically to exclude the ecology of an animal from their description of the animal itself. In such a scenario, imagine the elaborate, even outlandish accounts that would be generated trying to make sense of the giraffe's lengthy neck without being able to assume its correlative ecosystem of *trees*.

Such an infelicitous methodological situation proves to be the case for secular critical theory. For it is forced to account for what it means to be human, to account for basic human behavioral constants, such as ritual, worship, and sacrifice, while simultaneously excluding the vast majority of human ecology: the transcendent. The human environment is suffused with divinity. But anthropologists are forced to exclude human folk accounts of sacrifice and thus miss what in fact demands to be the case. Human beings sacrifice *because the gods demand it*. Following the chapter above on the divine economy, the Most High God provides a means for the gods to be fed by mortals. The problem is not this primordial arrangement of things. The problem is the mismanagement and aggrandizing of worship to themselves on the part of the gods. The fall twists an economy that was, at root, good.

Let us turn, then, to a theological anthropology: what human beings do is imitate, we engage in mimesis,[17] ritual being the paradigm case. "Monkey see, monkey do," and that is true for the primate who is also a little "lower than the angels" (Ps 8:5, quoted in Heb 2:7). We imitate, to the degree that it is possible, those heavenly realities *whose environment we share,* willy-nilly, but whom we cannot grasp (either in our hands, or with our minds). Human beings sacrifice because the gods demand it, for it is essential to human nature, as that hybrid angelic animal, to hold commerce with divinity. Sooner or later your god will consume you. For the fallen angels still possess angelic nature and still attempt a perverse imitation of God. The issue is not whether or not to sacrifice, but to which god, at what time, and after which manner.

Sacrifice is certainly foundational to society and culture. But, as per the previous chapter's exposition of liturgy and sacrifice as a gift economy mediating fellowship among unequals, sacrifice is not, at root, fundamentally violent. Violence is its perversion. Rabbi Moshe Halbertal[18] founds

---

16. See McGowan, "Eucharist and Sacrifice" and "Rehashing the Leftovers of Idols."

17. Here I want completely to agree with Girard.

18. See Halbertal, *On Sacrifice.*

his description of sacrifice not in some pre-historic conjecture, but in the biblical account of the first sacrifices: those of Cain and Abel. The violence is not in the sacrifice. The violence is not in the risk of sacrifice, the risk that the gift will be rejected. The violence comes as a result of the rejection of the gift *post facto*. Cain cannot bear that his is rejected while his brother's is accepted. The inequality created between peers, the reversal of firstborn priority, is too much to bear. And the result is violence—the first murder. Violence may be linked to sacrifice, after the fall. But they are simply not coterminous.[19]

Before the face of the infinite, whose gift to us is our very being, the only authentic response is total self-oblation.[20] From a philosophical-theological point of view, self-emptying opens the possibility of unity with the infinite. And as the giraffe communes with its environment through consuming the produce thereof, a human being longs for communion with the gods, and, ultimately, with the infinite One; and makes her meager attempt to do so through the consumption of the produce of our divinely-saturated environment in that ritual universal we know as sacrifice.

In their inability or unwillingness to see in sacrifice an enactment of finite longing for the infinite, secular reductionists also fail to see that sacrifice is not scapegoating, nor, in the main, atonement or propitiation for sin. Interestingly, only a holocaust/burnt offering is atoning. Sacrifice, in the main, is communion, the celebration of an economy of abundance.[21] Sacrifice, under conditions of grace, is not about death, but transformation.

19. Notwithstanding debates as to whether taking animal life constitutes violence, the mythos of the world engaged by Scripture is that higher has dominion over lower. Plant life was created on a day prior to the creation of animals and human beings. Thus, plant life provides the proper sustenance for animals and human beings. Animal and human life provide the proper sustenance for the gods (elohim). It is not violent for human beings to harvest and consume vegetables. Likewise, in the ANE, it is not violent for gods to harvest and consume human beings. Human beings and animals, however, were created on the same day. Thus, unless we are in service to the gods, it is illicit for human beings to take animal life. The only proper human slaughter and consumption of an animal is liturgical in nature—it is in service to the gods, for their consumption, and only thereafter potentially also consumed by human beings as a share granted to the god's human servants. It is, in a word, sacrifice. In the case of the people of God, it is sacrifice in service to, and when commanded, in fellowship with, the LORD.

20. Drawing on the tradition of English Platonic thought, I here follow Hedley's argument in a similar vein.

21. The following part of my reflection is based upon the work of Robert Daly, *Sacrifice Unveiled* and other works. I am thankful to Timothy Brunk here for pointing me in this direction and for his own work.

One life becomes another. One life is taken up into the life of another. A higher form of life transfigures a lower. Sacrifice, among other things, is always a gift from a lesser to a greater party inviting (further) relationship. Specifically, it is the gift of something to consume. Within this over-arching nature of sacrifice, it is also often a communion, a fellowship, a shared meal, a final consummation, a joyful feast of thanksgiving.[22] But it is all of these things and more because it is, more fundamentally, simultaneously an *imitatio angeli*, even *Dei*.[23] As the Most High has invited his sons to feast at his board (and, in some myths, provisioned by earthly sacrifice) so too Israel is invited to feast as a new counsel of 'elohim with the Most High God. God himself feasts on, enjoys, and dines with his people through sacrifice. The consumption of sacrificial offerings is a share in the divine nature. In all cases sacrifice is the gift to God of a consumable good.

Finally, and more seriously, the reduction of sacrifice to violence is rarely noted for the supersessionism, even, perhaps, anti-Semitism inherent to it. It seems that secular critical theory is unfamiliar with the solid tradition of scholarship on Old Testament sacrifice.[24] For sacrifice is assumed in Judaism and in the religion of ancient Israel. And the old covenant Scriptures assume its divine sanction and command.

OLD COVENANT SACRIFICE

Ancient Israel had an elaborate sacrificial economy of gracious substitution that the Christian Old Testament Scriptures describe as the direct command of God. Part of this system even includes a central scapegoating ritual, from which, of course, the modern term derives its name.[25] Christians need to be able to find a positive, rather than a reactive reading of this deep structure within our tradition. Otherwise, we teeter on the edge of other impermissible Christian reductions of Judaism: contributing to, rather

22. It could be argued that all sacrifice presumes a kind of communion, but ritually speaking, a holocaust is clearly only sweet smelling to the LORD and without even priestly sharing. The norm of experienced sacrifice for the average ancient Israelite, nevertheless, would have included some kind of communication, even if only priestly.

23. See Klawans, *Purity, Sacrifice*.

24. Allen P. Ross offers a summary of the scholarly literature up to the publication of his *Recalling the Hope of Glory*. The works of Margaret Barker and Jon Levenson push such scholarship further.

25. While the scapegoat is not technically sacrificed, the ritual as a whole includes three sacrifices and is clearly sacrificial in nature.

than abstaining from, the cycle of secular anti-Semitism. For it is thematic for the Scriptures that in sacrifice God demands the entire person. And this scriptural theme coheres with the philosophical theology of sacrifice described above: oblation of the earthly for communion with the heavenly, sublimation of the visible for fellowship with the invisible, self-oblation of the finite for union with the infinite.

One way to read the narrative arc of the old covenant, even the entire Scriptures, is that it is about the worship of the living God and its correction and therapy. The old covenant is therefore deeply concerned with sacrifice, sacrificial correction and therapy. Even sacrificial therapy, which is to say, both the therapy of sacrifice and therapy through sacrifice.[26] As the narrative of the old covenant Scriptures unfold, we see an initial demand for total self-oblation turn to a series of dispensations from this demand as it comes to mean certain death for the oblationer, given the human condition after the fall. Eden itself, as a garden, is a temple environment. The garden temple of Eden forms a perfect human temple, with its human servants being both priests and victims in the living "service" that forms perfect, pre-fallen self-oblation.[27]

All life, and therefore all human life, is a gift from God.[28] And gifts must circulate. Daughters are "given" in marriage, providing progeny for another tribe, clan, or family. Sons carry the father's name, the tribal name. Sons return as gifts to God. The (firstborn) son was accepted as substitute for the father in ANE religion.[29] In Scripture, God establishes a ritual substitution for the firstborn: circumcision (Gen 17 and Exod 4:26). With circumcision, we are now two substitutes away from the original demand: total self-oblation.[30] Another example is that of the Nazirite vow and temple service (Num 6:5). It is not clear whether at one point these were simply the same thing or not, but they are clearly closely related. The child need not

---

26. I am indebted to correspondence with John Milbank for the terminology of "therapy."

27. See Ross, *Recalling the Hope*. The word translated for "working" the garden in the Eden narrative is identical to that which is translated "service" with regard to the duties of the priests and Levites in the tabernacle and temple. That same word is translated *leitourgia*, and its related morphemes, in the LXX.

28. See Hyde, *The Gift*, 121–41.

29. See Levenson, *Death and Resurrection*.

30. Although circumcision is chronologically prior in the biblical narrative, it does not alter the ritual logic. The testing of Abraham simply calls him to make good on his pledge: total oblation of the firstborn.

actually be slaughtered; he may be dedicated to perpetual temple service—a "living sacrifice." The prophet and priest, Samuel, presents a key scriptural example. In this, we get closer to a return to Edenic sacrifice: living service, rather than self-immolation. Finally, there is the establishment of the Levitical priesthood as a substitute for all the firstborn of Israel (Num 3). Again, a substitute for a substitute. Within this Levitical code, the firstborn would be redeemed with two turtledoves or pigeons (Lev 1:14); yet another substitute within an economy already overflowing with substitution. But this is no mere *representational* substitution. The substitute *participates* in the thing substituted, thus, through fidelity, manifesting an ontologically thick pledge of the original. The substitute is sacrament.

Most cultures classify human life as a gift bestowed by the gods or God. In many traditional societies, including the ones recalled by biblical texts, women are given by a corporate body (such as a tribe, clan, or family) to another corporate body, for its continuation. The corporate body must have wombs in order to continue. Men, then, are given to the gods, or God, by the corporate body for a return gift on life itself. God accepts the firstfruits passed back in a divine gift economy.[31] As per the previous chapter, the sacrificial system of the old covenant, as a whole, is a grand divine-human gift-cycle. Within that concourse, different sacrifices achieve different functions. A key and central portion of that gift economy is the grace-filled system of substitutions for the firstborn. No human life is literally slaughtered—although it is certainly continuously sacrificed, mimetically, ritually, through substitution. For example, Abraham and the sacrifice of Isaac, God the Father and the sacrifice of his Son, Jesus Christ—the focus of this chapter.

When God exacts his final plague upon Egypt he only takes what is his own, he only calls in on his claim on the firstborn. This demand of the firstfruits (and thus firstborn) itself represents a generous dispensation from the total demand: *all* life. "All things come of thee and of thine own have we given thee" (1 Chr 29:14 AV). So, in Exodus, the gentile nation that refuses to recognize him nevertheless miraculously pays tribute to the true Lord of Heaven and Earth. It is a story of sacrifice, of sacrificial therapeutics. In the final plague, the LORD provides Egypt therapuetical correction of its idolatry.

---

31. See Hyde, *The Gift*, 121–41. Interestingly, Christianity, as per Augustine, turns *females* into *males* for female martyrdom (sacrifice to God), which is just as valuable and acceptable a gift of the firstfruits as is that of male martyrdom.

I have said that substitution is only necessary after the fall. And I believe this is true in its most technical sense. However, in order to have the communion with God that is our end, the imbalance of transcendence must somehow be offset—even had there been no fall. For example, how can we give a gift of gratitude back to God equal to his gift to us? Only through total self-sacrifice. Now, granted, prior to the fall I would argue that total oblation would be an everlasting life of reasonable service. But even an *everlasting* finite life cannot match the infinitude of the gift of being itself. Thus, at an ontological level, the demand for substitution itself may well be prior to the fall, indeed, natural to our humanity. The substitution of gift for gift from God may well be the atmosphere we breathe to sing our song of thanks.

Substitutionary atonement thus reuses that fundamental gift of substitution, swallowing up the breach we made when in our presumption we pretended not to need the primordial substitute. For is that not the very over-reaching of the fall? We thought it meet to grasp, for the fruit was within our reach. If we need substitution to return the gift that leads to fellowship across the finite to infinite interval, how can we possibly achieve that donation that is sufficient to restart that economy once lost due to the fall? Thanks be to God; the Son "did not consider divinity as something to be grasped. But he emptied himself . . . even to death on the cross. Therefore God also highly exalted him" (Phil 2:6–9). Sacrificial atonement is given as a gift of God exceeding all previous giving, in order to correct an error, make right a wrong, clean a pollution, heal an illness, all due to the fall—and restore communion, fellowship, economy, flow. Christ's substitutionary atonement achieves its end because it fits into the larger, pre-fallen "natural" economy of God and his house, the cosmos.

ATONEMENT

There is within the old covenant Scriptures what appears to be a strong critique of this whole sacrificial system in the so-called oracular[32] prophets and scattered throughout the Psalter. This can often be over-played by Christian and especially Protestant exegetes. The problem with sacrifice was not the eating of animals, the unequal economy of gift-exchange be-

---

32. I say so-called because it has been a consistent tradition within the critical reading of Scripture vastly to separate oracular from apocalyptic prophecy, rather than recognize them as two different literary modes within a shared world-project.

tween God and human beings, nor the system of interlocking substitution in itself, but its use, or, rather, *abuse*, resulting from a detachment, through infidelity, of the participant from the total demand to which the substitutes offered temporary deferral in one sense, and a foretaste of the pledge (even, of resurrection)[33] in another.[34] That is to say, what God rejects is perfunctory performance without the "thickness" of total self-oblation and the expectation of transcendent contact we call faith. The fall affects all things natural to being human, sacrifice included.

Take for example Psalm 50's demand to "offer to God a sacrifice of thanksgiving" (v. 14). After its (seeming to modern eyes) diatribe against the sacrificial system, the psalmist is not indicating that the performer of the psalm ought simply to "say grace," and not bother with all those animals. Rather, Psalm 50 enjoins the worshiper to offer one of the *prescribed* sacrifices: the *todah* sacrifice.[35] This is the sacrifice that acknowledges salvation from a dire predicament or situation and is associated with the fulfillment of a vow after the Lord had answered a petition for salvation from the predicament. It involved bread, wine, and the slaughter and communal eating of an animal. It involved the proclamation on the part of the one fulfilling her vow of a psalm of thanksgiving moving from lament to gratitude for salvation from that which was lamentable, Psalm 22 being a key example of such a psalm, and the narrative of Hannah and Samuel (1 Sam 1ff.) as a paradigmatic pericope.

Psalm 50 is not "letting someone off the hook" of the sacrificial system. It is focusing on a particular sacrifice that is the least likely to be performed perfunctorily, for it is the result of the fulfillment of a vow made in crisis and in celebration of deliverance therefrom. Psalm 50 prioritizes the fulfillment of vows over the holocaust and other sacrifices that do not directly result in communion. The sacrifice the Lord desires is "a broken and contrite heart" (Ps 51:17), beating inside a body performing the appointed sacrifice, whose mouth speaks out thanksgiving, and with whom the Lord grants communion: table fellowship.

How do we deal, then, with what seems to be a central contradiction of the old covenant Scriptures: God simultaneously demands and detests

---

33. See Levenson, *Death and Resurrection*.

34. See Klawans, *Purity, Sacrifice*.

35. The sacrifice of thanksgiving first appears in Lev 22:29 and appears again in Ps 116:17. Jonah 2:9 also mentions it: "But I with the voice of thanksgiving will sacrifice to you." For a summary of the scholarship see Chapter 17 of Allen Ross's *Recalling the Hope*.

sacrifice?[36] The answer is that God wants the full oblation of every person, and through that, communion, fellowship, with those whom he has made.[37] The demand for animal and other sacrifice is actually not so much a command as a concession to human need. God will gladly take the substitute if it is given truly as a pledge of such substitution: a true pledge of one's total abandon to God and God's will. Problems arise only when the LORD finds hypocrisy. The prophetic rejection of sacrifice is the rejection of a given, specific act, not the rejection of an entire system. It is customary prophetic hyperbole for the rejection of sacrifice's occasional hypocritical superfluity.[38]

The liturgy revealed in the old covenant represents a divine therapy in at least two senses. It provides a system of substitution that prevents immediate (human) death as the result of full self-oblation. It also provides a means of human transformation of the will through a sacrifice freed from idolatry. All other gods consume to our detriment. Only the God revealed in Scripture brings about the final consummation to our benefit.

Critical theory's most recently maligned sacrifice of the old covenant system is the so-called *scapegoat*[39] or, rather, the Day of Atonement sacrifice. Leviticus 16 presents one of the clearest and most dramatic descriptions of liturgical action in the old covenant canon. If we read Leviticus 16 liturgically, through the lens of liturgical theology and anthropology, understanding the primacy of behavior and performance, we are struck by the total lack of any myth that corresponds to this ritual.[40] For, interestingly, in many places, historical and tribal etiologies are provided on top of the obvious cosmological symbolism. But no etiologies are given for the Day of Atonement.[41]

36. See Congar, *At the Heart of Christian Worship*, where this question is also posed.

37. I am grateful to Tarah van de Weile who pointed out to me that my argument here is a Christian parallel to that of the rabbinic argument (namely, Yochanon ben Zakkai's) for the shift from animal sacrifice to prayer at the temple hours counting as the sacrifice of Israel under conditions of diaspora. God still demands sacrifice. But he is willing to accept total self-oblation under many forms so long as it is faithful.

38. See Klawans, *Purity, Sacrifice*.

39. Again, I refer here to work of René Girard.

40. That is to say, a myth that is directly attested in Scripture. The myth runs as a vein through all of Scripture: one is, or seems to be, rejected, that another may be elevated. These are often twins, or brothers of the same mother. The narrative often also involves the reversal of traditional birth-order rights. Again, see Levenson's *Death and Resurrection*.

41. And yet, the theme of the twin, and the descent and restoration of one gone down

The temple provided an environment for enacting ritual participation in cosmic, and cosmos-rendering, events. Space does not allow me to discuss the cosmic correspondence between ANE cosmology and the ritual actions, architecture, and furnishings of the temple.[42] Suffice it to say, that Leviticus 16 corresponds roles of priests and high priest (Aaron) to holy place (visible heavens) and most holy place (invisible heavens) spatially on the one hand, and the daily to the yearly, temporally, on the other.[43] The high priest prepares for this unique ritual action by atoning first for himself and his family. Once prepared for such ritual action, he puts off his usual high priestly attire and puts on, for this one day of the year only, pure white linen. Upon his turban, he places a golden plate with the Divine Name inscribed upon it. Two identical goats are selected. Lots are cast. One of these identical twins is designated *as* the LORD and the other *as* Azazel.[44] Azazel is driven out of the camp, outside the city gates. The goat who is as the LORD is slaughtered and his blood used to renew the tabernacle-temple, starting from the Most Holy Place and working outwards, or, rather, *downwards*. Upon completing the cleansing of the temple, the high priest emerges again, lifts up his hands and blesses the people.

We will take up the Day of Atonement again, in Chapter Four, when we discuss the book of Hebrews and the figural reading of Scripture. But for now, what is the myth that corresponds to this ritual? What is the theology

---

to Sheol is a recurring theme that manifests throughout the Old Testament Scriptures (and New Testament, for that matter) and especially the Torah, even granting a uniting pattern to the literary material of, say, Genesis, with the more ritual and legal material to follow.

42. I hope to explore this more deeply in further work dedicated to a liturgical meditation upon particulars of the old covenant economy.

43. By which, I mean that while priests enter the holy place daily, only the high priest can enter the holy of holies, and that only once each year.

This description relies upon the exegesis of these passages provided by Margaret Barker's imaginative old covenant scholarship, found especially in her *Temple Themes in Christian Worship*. Barker draws from pseudopigrapha such as *Enoch*, and authoritative Jewish works such as the Mishna to make these connections. See also Fletcher-Louis, *Jesus Monotheism*. Fletcher-Louis develops a temple-cosmos approach to the Bible and Second Temple Jewish literature similar to that of Barker's, but some would find his approach more grounded.

44. What, or *who* is Azazel? The very scapegoat ritual that Girard uses to name his own theory may not itself have represented a "scapegoat" ritual. Many translations render the word "for" rather than "as" the Lord and Azazel. Margaret Barker regards this as a theologically-motivated mistranslation. These animals ritually enact the Lord and Azazel respectively.

of this liturgy? I would like to argue that, for Christian theology, the answer corresponds to the previous question: over what liturgy, what sacrifice, does Jesus Christ preside?

JESUS'S SACRIFICE

The terms of the new covenant meet our fundamental anthropological needs and conditions, rather than abolishing or changing them. God does not despise our nature. He creates, takes, and works with it. Indeed, our very nature makes us fit for communion with God. The liturgy of the new temple is also, therefore, a liturgy of sacrifice.[45] The new covenant does, however, radically change the system of substitution from that of the covenant mediated through Moses. God performs the perfect human oblation for himself by sacrificing himself to himself through, as, and in being human. The performance of this sacrifice is conditioned upon the *shalom*, the peacefulness of the Triune liturgy.

Before the fall we must presume that full sacrifice would not mean death, but rather self-sublimation in the ecstasy, the "standing outside one-self" of perfect union with God, perfect grounding of "self" outside the self in the only self-grounded One. After the fall, however, full sacrifice would come to mean annihilation of the individual human instance. Hence the Old Testament system of substitution constitutes a form of grace.

Jesus, as fully human and yet fully divine, fulfills the originary demand of total self-oblation to the infinite One and, in the face of the death inherent to the fall, he is able to do so because he is the Living One: "I was dead, and see, I am alive forever and ever" (Rev 1:18). Resurrection is the "better promise" (Heb 8:6) of the new covenant, delivered by the Father to Jesus as the firstfruits of those who are being saved (1 Cor 15:20). Jesus

---

45. See Lathrop, *Holy Things*, which contains strong statements denying that Jesus' death or the Christian divine service is sacrifice in any way. But he qualifies this, carefully, with the adverb "literally" (140). Coming from different traditions and using different theological vocabulary I am inclined, not to downplay our differences, but still to recognize that much may be semantic in nature. I, too, wish to deny that Jesus' death or the divine service is literally sacrifice. I assert that they are *more* than literal sacrifice, they are *anagogical* sacrifice. Further engagement would require another chapter, so I must unfortunately stop this important digression. I hope to take it up again more fully at another occasion.

Christ willingly sacrificed himself in love of his Father and, in that love, for the life of the world (John 6:51).[46]

Theories of Jesus' death that make him *merely* a hapless victim, however historically probable from a secular point of view, actually do violence to the Gospel narrative and the liturgical traditions of the church.[47] One can only see Jesus' life, death, and resurrection as sacrifice in a *mystery*, through apocalypse. On earth, the confused disciples see only the bungled trial and execution of an innocent man. But in apocalyptic vision, the faithful have revealed before them the mystery hidden from the foundation of the earth (Eph 1:4): the archetype of the firstfruits, of the *todah*, of the Day of Atonement, of the Passover has become incarnate: "Alleluia, Christ our Passover is sacrificed for us."[48] The sacrifice of Jesus Christ is the sacrifice he himself performs, willingly: Christ the victim, Christ the priest,[49] concluding the sacrificial system of substitution. The sacrifice of Jesus Christ entails at least three things about the nature of the new covenant.

First, the new covenant of Jesus Christ does not end sacrifice in and of itself, for it does not end but rather re-starts God's gracious gift-cycle economy with his creation. Nor does Jesus' sacrifice abolish old covenant sacrifice in the sense of its mere erasure. Jesus Christ culminates the elaborate system of substitution. Jesus is that paradoxical substitute that is not a substitute. The paradox of Jesus' sacrifice is that the substitute for all was the only sacrifice that was ever, fully, no substitute in any way, but that very substitute that, nevertheless, allows for our own full and original self-sacrifice, again.

Jesus substitutes for Israel, even for Adam, while offering no substitute for himself in the face of the Father's demand of total self-oblation. In so doing, his perfect non-substitution ends the cycle of substitution and provides a new, non-substitutionary sacrificial system (this is the new covenant) as a means for those within his corporate body to offer themselves in full self-oblation without (necessarily) actual, this-worldly, physical death. Christians become, through Christ, a living sacrifice.

46. This passage from John is then quoted in the Anaphora of St. Chrysostom.

47. See Peterson, "What Happened?" In this article, Peterson argues that the paradoxical relationship of Jesus being handed-over through the betrayal of Judas and his own willingly handing himself over are essential to the Gospel narrative. Liturgical translations that smooth out this mutual allusion do injustice to this paradox within the biblical narrative.

48. The Book of Common Prayer, 364, which alludes to 1 Cor 5:7–8.

49. See 1982 Hymnal, Hymn #174.

The church has always honored martyrdom as perfect participation in Christ. Martyrdom performs the paradigm of Christian sacrifice: Christ's paschal mystery. Human desire is mimetic: "Monkey see, monkey do." Christians see their Lord and desire to take up their cross and follow him. This may mean literal death for the sake of Christ. But it may mean a life of self-oblation in preparation for this final "moment of Christian witness."[50] The new covenant solution to death in oblation is to provide the perfect means to re-enable total self-oblation without *immediate* corporal death: participation in the resurrected Lord. Our witness in martyrdom is our most pure liturgy, our most pure divine service as Christians, as human beings. We participate in and anticipate our own martyrdom in a life of self-oblation. This is what the church recognizes when she recognizes the pattern of Christ in the saints. Finally, the ritual behavior of the Christian mysteries, and, especially in this case, that of baptism, perform a ritual mimesis and share in the paschal mystery of Christ, and the Christian's own witness, martyrdom. Thus, we find a kind of new covenant system of substitution.

Second, the new covenant represents a new system, so to speak, *without* substitution, arising in the earthly, human time following the incarnation and paschal mystery of the living God. Jesus is not simply *our* substitute, but he who enables our own perfect self-offering, in, through, and as "living members incorporate"[51] of his body. Once the perfect human sacrifice is made, all other sacrifice, *as substitution*, becomes obsolete. Christians actually find themselves back in the same position before God as that of humanity before the Abrahamic covenant, in some ways even Edenic. The specific laws that enable the corporate body of Israel, God's firstborn son, to live in gift economy together are in some sense no longer necessary under conditions of the new covenant, for a more primordial anthropological condition reemerges. But this is possible, of course, only in Jesus' fulfillment, never abrogation, of the Torah. God demands total human self-offering. Due to the fall, the only acceptable sacrifice is that of Jesus, a "blood that speaks a better word than the blood of Abel" (Heb 12:24).

Third, the new covenant liturgy is therefore a liturgy that, rather than offering substitution, offers the capacity for total participation in self-oblation *without* death, rather, resurrection: "Blessed are those who are invited

---

50. See Balthasar, *Moment of Christian Witness*.

51. The Book of Common Prayer, 339.

to the marriage supper of the Lamb" (Rev 19:9). And, because in Jesus God gives the gift of infinitude, the sacrifice of Jesus satisfies the fundamental ontological need for substitution. Recently, it has proved popular to dismiss *penal substitutionary atonement*. I agree that the *penal* aspect of it makes little sense, as ancient sacrifice had nothing to do with punishment. But to dismiss that Jesus' sacrifice is substitutionary dismisses out of hand an essential aspect of Christ's work and perhaps even basic needs for relationship across the interval of Creator to creature. The substitution of Jesus (corporal body) grounds the satisfaction of the church (the corporate body of Christ). So these theories are not opposed.

Our very selves are gifts of the infinite absolute Source. Thus, our sacrifice is *our very selves*, our souls and bodies. Within the gift economy of grace this self-sacrifice is self-sublimation, not annihilation. After the fall, sacrifice itself becomes infected with the disease of scarcity. Competition and scarcity reduce self-sacrifice to self-annihilation. When we are out of the flow of the economy, bloated with unreturned gift, any attempt to re-start the flow from the human side alone results in death. But if the sacrifice does not come from the one who stopped the flow, it cannot genuinely return that reality to the flow. We find ourselves trapped. We need a ransom.

God reverses the affects of the fall through the incarnation and paschal mystery of the Word of God in Jesus Christ. Jesus is the re-start of the gift economy, the flow. For it is the ultimate gift: the gift of God himself to humanity that is also, simultaneously, a human gift to God.[52] We should find familiar this language about a gift that is simultaneously from God to human being and from being human to God. An economic anagogy repositions our inheritance from Anselm, and even the so-called *ransom theory* he repudiated.[53] Positioning the economy of salvation within the economy of gift grants us insight into Anselm's account of atonement by enlarging our typical late Western interpretive context. Anselm's intuition sits within ANE terms recovered in Scripture's mythomorphic context.

The problem of our current cultural logic is that we make scarcity and competition primordial. In this gift economic account, we find an economic substitutionary atonement, rather than a penal substitutionary atonement. Furthermore, we have an economic *ransom*, rather than a release from a

---

52. This gets us underneath Girard, so to speak. Girard gives an accurate account of sacrifice outside of grace and under fallen conditions, where scarcity and competition reign. But Girard fails to make sense of the place of sacrifice in an economy of abundance, communion, and gift.

53. See Anselm, *Cur Deus homo*.

kidnapping on the part of the devil. The ransom is that of the Year of Jubilee, the cancellation of debt, the return to promised land.

If we remove living knowledge of the behavioral context, we lose the intuitive, lived, tacit link between inherited discourse (the Scriptures) and the event (revelation, theophany) that inspired it. I propose that a gift economy composed a significant portion of that encounter and its subsequent behavior. Retrieving gift retrieves a missing frame.

Anselm translated gift economy into his contemporary gift economic media: baronial honor and its courts.[54] It is in many ways an apt and even organic analogue to the gift economy and politics of the ANE.[55] By the time we get to our day, the context of honor is lost in much of Western society and we move to the next nearest thing for us: a court of law—even nation-state, code-based, criminal law. Thus penal substitutionary atonement is born. But this translation is less organic and less apt than that of Anselm's in his day—and far more misleading as to the divine nature and economy.

We are now in a position, thanks to some sound anthropology and historiography, to get underneath the cultural matrix assumed by Anselm, or, at least, to situate his analogy better, within an ANE world of gift-exchange as definitive even of honor and politics. Although substitutionary, Anselm's atonement is not penal. Anselm pitches his account in the key of the gift-exchange of his day: honor and dishonor.

It is because of scarcity and competition, not sacrifice per se, that violence arises.[56] In fact, if anything, scarcity and competition exactly mark the loss of a sacrificial economy. The liturgy of the benefactor encompasses the gift returned in sacrifice. The damage incurred and accumulated (unto ages of ages) of all this violence is, nevertheless, and thankfully, something God can sublimate—that is the good news. Gift economies demand a primordial, grounding donation. The sacrifice of the Logos is that donation *in illo tempore*—and becomes for us that donation again, in response to the

---

54. See Hart, "A Gift Exceeding."

55. Anselm even remembered the angels in his account of atonement. Anselm explains that God's perfect cosmic liturgy suffered due to the fall of the angels. The covenantal economy with human being becomes, then, an "*elohim* replacement project." God fills out the full number, or, perhaps, relationship, ratio, of created persons to complete his cosmic liturgy. See Anselm, *Cur Deus Homo*, 125–34.

56. See Tanner, *Jesus*, 67–95. Using an economic analogy, Tanner gives a wonderful correction to traditional theories of atonement in order to develop a theory of atonement that moves us away from penal substitution. Grounded in her reflections, I move explicitly into the narrative of gift economics, and, thereby, bring back substitution without penalty.

fall ("who for us and for our salvation came down from heaven"), incarnate and grounded on earth.

What then is the liturgy over which Jesus presides as great high priest? Jesus presides over the cosmic liturgy in the heavenly places as God's Son and as priest of the cosmos. The cosmic and angelic liturgy described in the previous chapter has a presiding priest, even Jesus Christ our Lord, the Word incarnate. The incarnation and pashcal mystery are the earthly manifestation, the "touchdown point" of that sempiternal reality on earth, in our visible and temporal continuum. The priest must come to the altar (the earth, the visible, the sensible) in order to offer the victim (himself). What looks like the bungled trial and execution of an innocent man becomes, through apocalyptic vision, and the knowledge that comes by faith, the revelation of the sacrifice of God for the eternal covenant in the heavenly places. That eternal sacrifice manifests, perennially, in the Eucharist of the faithful. The primordial donation once lost is now restored, and in Christ's corporate body, the church has its share and makes its humble sacrifice.

THE RITUAL MYSTERIES AND EUCHARISTIC SACRIFICE

The ritual mysteries provide the means by which we share in the economy of Christ when actual martyrdom is not immediately available: baptism and the divine service ritually participate in Jesus' death, and in and through that, each Christian's own martyrdom: "and here we offer and present unto thee, O Lord, our selves, our souls and bodies."[57] They also grant a share in Jesus' resurrection and therein and thereby the Christian's own. So, first and foremost, the Christian's participation in Jesus' sacrifice is a life of total dedication to God, a "living sacrifice;" and that to the point of willingness to accept its total actualization in martyrdom.[58] No one, when building a tower, fails "first [to] sit down and estimate the cost" (Luke 14:28). ("Tower," here serves as circumlocution for the temple.)

Now, ritual is behavioral analogy. It is the behavior to which theology provides an adequate discursive counterpart. The sacrifice of Jesus Christ is the most *apropos* place to use the word "sacrifice." It is not only *analogically appropriate* to use the term "sacrifice" for the life of Jesus, but actually anagogically revealed to be its most appropriate instance. All other sacrifice and all other uses of the word "sacrifice" form either an appropriate analogue

57. The Book of Common Prayer, 336.

58. See Balthasar, *Moment of Christian Witness.*

(as in old and new covenant worship) or an inappropriate perversion or misconstrual of the practice (as in idolatry) and its concomitant discourse (as in the language of "sacrifice" in modern warfare, etc.).[59] Through the mystery of the Gospels, the human trial and death of an innocent man from Nazareth is now the sacrifice of God, the ritual of the heavenly places. Apocalypse becomes narrative anagogy. That is to say, the narrative structure of apocalyptic discourse is anagogy for transcendent dynamics. Biblical apocalyptic performs an anagogy upon the mythic structures of the Mediterranean basin in general, and the ANE in particular. So, for example, contrary to some recent approaches, apocalyptic is not so much the revelation of *nonviolence* as the revelation of the *sublimation of violence*: behold the Lamb who was slain has begun to reign (Rev 5). Without this acknowledgement we cannot consider the depth of importance that books such as Revelation and Hebrews represent in the New Testament and in the Christian tradition.[60]

Peeling back layers of theological allegory, illustrative symbolism, and simple (Protestant and) modern embarrassment over the straightforward meaning of the ritual action of the divine service the fundamental anthropological analogy is clear: the ritual eating of a ritual (god-)man. It is a ritual eating of a man who has *become* ritual in "this holy and bloodless sacrifice."[61] But who is doing the eating? God or human being(s)? And who is being eaten? God or human being? This is the paradox of communion and consummation. Jesus, the God-man, becomes the ritual of divine-human concourse. And in so becoming, passes on the life of the age to come, resurrection life.

This paradox is the ritual therapy that corresponds to the conditions of the new covenant. Instead of a system of substitution that *prevents* immediate (human) death Christians have a ritual participation *in* Jesus' death and freedom from death in resurrection. Absolutely continuous with its old covenant inheritance, the ritual therapy of the new covenant provides a means of human transformation of the will by freeing sacrifice from idolatry. God brings about the final consummation in the ritual action of

---

59. See Halbertal, *On Sacrifice.*

60. Hedley, *Sacrifice Imagined,* 18.

61. St. Chrysostom's anaphora.

communion. "You are what you eat:[62] "that we may evermore dwell in him, and he in us."[63]

It is important here briefly to note that the impulse of Protestants to reject the sacrifice of the mass has truth in it. The sacrifice is complete and in the most important sense unrepeatable at the event of the paschal mystery itself: something that occurred in time and space on the earthly plane of reality. The Catholic impulse to emphasize the sacrifice of the mass also has truth in it. The divine service fully participates and manifests Jesus' sacrifice. At the time of the Reformation we lacked the retrieval of the Eucharistic Prayer, an understanding that thanksgiving is what consecrates, and the sense that the entire paschal mystery saves, and not just the cross and passion. We were therefore, in the West, forced to decide between a nominalistic historicizing of salvation on the one hand, or an Aristotelian substantial repetition on the other.[64]

The challenge of the Liturgical Renewal of the twentieth century, to both sides of our sad Western division, is that it speaks as a corrective to both extremes. It may turn out to be the case that neither Protestants nor Catholics maintained a sound theology of Eucharistic sacrifice—where immanent reductions on both sides flattened what is actually a nested set of patterns crossing various media and levels of reality. Renewal opens the door for retrieving thanksgiving, paschal mystery, and, therefore, liturgy as an entire ritual performance. And in these fundamental insights of liturgical renewal we can discern divine service as full ritual participation in the paschal mystery, and sacrifice as joyful communion through total self-oblation, a festival meal.

CONCLUSION

If the liturgy is the cosmic economy, then what liturgical theology engages when it attempts to discern the "Eucharistic sacrifice" is not primarily an

---

62. Schmemann turns this line from Feuerbach on its head in *For the Life of the World*, 11.

63. *The Book of Common Prayer*, 337.

64. Although Luther almost totally rejected any language of sacrifice around the communion service, and Calvin would admit it, but only with circumspection, the Anglican tradition within Protestantism never rejected language of sacrifice with regard to the divine service. This is due in no small part to the devotional material of Jeremy Taylor, see especially "The Heavenly Sacrifice and Earthly Sacraments." Here I follow Byron Stuhlman's summary in his *A Good and Joyful Thing*.

engagement with any one particular local or historic human ritual action, but Jesus Christ's sacrifice that restarts the cosmic liturgy in the face of the fall—Jesus' atonement, his economic substitution.

Liturgical theology is thus, in one of its most proper senses, the sacrifice of Jesus Christ. By derivation, participation, and direct implication, liturgical theology is also a given life of total Christian witness. Christ enables full self-sacrifice without substitution through the promise of resurrection, thus rendering martyrdom the fullest participation in the cosmic rite. By like derivation, liturgical theology is the Christian ritual mysteries enacted in baptism and the divine service. For the divine service is the life and paschal mystery of Jesus Christ, the life of the Christian by, with, in, and through Jesus Christ, and the life of the church, Christ's body corporate, in her liturgy. So, echoing down nested continua and transferring across various media liturgical theology is a gift-cycle economy of familial relationship with God.

At a further remove, then, liturgical theology is discourse *concerning* the sacrifice of Jesus Christ and the way in which, by mystery, the faithful participate this liturgy, both ritually and, most importantly, in Christian life. Liturgical theology contemplates the way in which these realities (Christ's life, work, and paschal mystery, the Christian life of discipleship, and the church's life of liturgical worship) overlap, blend, inform, and empower one another. Thus, the next chapter takes the sacrifice of Jesus Christ as the "nest" in which we find the gift of human salvation and its noetic counterpart, contemplation.

Chapter Three

Liturgical Theology as Contemplation of Mystery

How can we enjoy the new economy of Jesus in God? Our human, earthly liturgy initiates us into the mystery of Christ. The focus of this chapter is the way in which *anthropos* nests within the cosmos—and finds restoration through the donation of Christ. Human salvation and its noetic counterpart, contemplation, nests within the economy of the sacrifice of Jesus Christ. Liturgical theology, therefore, does not so much refer to subjective reflection on immanent rituals and ritualizations, but extends the Christian mystery and its ritual initiation into human contemplation and discourse. In this chapter, I will first explore theology as contemplation. Then I will turn to liturgy as mystery before combining the two in a definition of liturgical theology as contemplation of mystery.

THEOLOGY AS CONTEMPLATION

Theology as an activity indicates contemplation. If theology is divine pattern recognition, then contemplation names this pattern recognition as a kind of psychic or noetic act or behavior. The goal of contemplation is the union of the soul with God. Now divine union, or, *theosis*, is not merely a noetic or psychic event. Theosis encompasses the human being entire: corporate, corporal, somatic, and psychic. Noetic illumination is, nevertheless, a part of full psychosomatic, ontological union wherein contemplation is the soul's attention to God. Contemplation is thus an inherent sign and means of the process of theosis.

74

The Christian tradition affirms a God who *is* contemplation. God is the perfect perichoresis in contemplative union of Father, Son, and Holy Spirit. Contemplation is that behavior that renders us most like God, enabling contact with and knowledge of God. Furthermore, contemplation is the logical grounds of the possibility of any revelation—including authoritative and scriptural.

God makes the human body the perfect medium for receiving the Word. Like a radio receiver that has been broken or mistuned, the human body needs to be tuned up to receive the signal it was built to receive, to perceive the world as it actually is. There is nothing inherently wrong with a broken, detuned radio receiver. But it may take some work to repair and retune it. That work is the spiritual gift of discipline: ascesis and liturgy. Retuning the human body enables the return of genuine human perception of the sensible and knowledge of the intelligible. Discipline allows the body to become less an obstacle to, and more a receptacle or conduit of, reality.

Because we encounter our embodiment as human beings along a continuum of corporal to corporate, by direct and organic analogy what holds for ascesis as the discipline of the corporal body holds for liturgy as the discipline of the corporate body. We thus extend this analogy to liturgy as, among other things, the corporate analog of ascesis, a perspective on Christian liturgical action as a shared, corporate embodied discipline, the expected gift at the end of which is corporate contemplative contact with the living God.

Ascesis and liturgy thus form a behavioral continuum corresponding to the somatic continuum, ranging from its corporal to its corporate manifestations. Ascesis[1] is the form that corporal contemplation takes, and is, in fact, its physical and embodied manifestation, e.g., prayer, meditation, fasting, alms-giving, confession, direction, and all as part of a repetitive rule of life, etc.[2]

---

1. Fagerberg, *Liturgical Asceticism.*

2. I present the above within that stream of the Christian tradition that understands mystical experience as the gift of contemplation, the expected end of all ascetic behavior. This is as opposed to that tradition that would separate mystical from ascetical theology. I see mystical theology as a part of ascetical theology in general because contemplative encounter with God is the gift to be expected from the genuine pursuit of Christian ascesis—much as the presence of Christ is expected as a part of the valid execution of the liturgy. See also my book: *Theology as Ascetic Act: Disciplining Christian Discourse*, where I argue that the disciplining of Christian discourse not only mirrors the disciplining of Christian bodies, but is itself in fact a part of such discipline, as discourse for human being is always an embodied act.

If contemplation is the natural state of the human mind, why do we find contemplation so difficult? Due to our unhealthy condition after the fall, the somatic continuum of human embodiment demands a set of therapeutic practices that analogically correspond to its varying needs of healing. So we find an ascetic-liturgical continuum of therapeutic practice, discipleship, or ascesis for the corporal body, and liturgy for the corporate body. Our corporeal Christian bodies engage *ascesis as their liturgy*, the ritual shaping of the body corporeal. The corporate Christian body engages *liturgy as its ascesis*—worship that shapes the body corporate. In both cases, we have ritual, repetitive, *mimetic* behavior, for our ritual and ascetic behavior performs an *imitatio Christi*. In both cases, we have discipline, which is to say, concrete teaching, which shapes and tunes up the body to practice, as if by second nature, the behavior native to its *telos*—union with God.

The shared goal of both ascesis and liturgy is preparation for the reception of the gift of contemplative union with God. But ascesis and liturgy engage the somatic continuum, and are not in a contrastive dialectical relationship with one another. The two go hand in hand. The initiate is a ready disciple of Christ. The Christian disciple is devoted to the church as the body corporate and to her liturgy. Together his or her mystical vision is honed and formed in the theological body—be that corporate, corporal, or, ideally, both.[3]

CONTEMPLATION AND MYSTICAL EXPERIENCE

I would like briefly to distinguish what the Christian tradition calls *contemplation* from the more modern concern for "mystical experience." One of the beneficial outcomes of this chapter is the ability to address problems of empiricist reduction of religious experience, mystical encounter, and prophetic knowledge. Mystical experience, insofar as it is Christian mystical experience, is always a gift from God received by rendering the human being a vessel for the gift. The Spirit's gift of the *vita activa* renders us worthy vessels of the same. The gift cannot be forced, only invited. But, again, as with the ritual mysteries, the gift is the expected result of the discipline,

3. See Dru Johnson, *Knowledge by Ritual*, where he likens the relationship of ritual to faith and knowledge using the analogy of a stereograph. At first, one must trust the "catechesis" of strange behaviors that lead to the revelation of the three-dimensional image hidden in what appears to be random lines. Once one has finally discerned the means of finding these images, each subsequent stereograph becomes easier to discern.

due not to human works, but to divine promise. Consequently, mystical experience outside of the life of Christian ascesis and liturgy is never fully trustworthy to the church and that for obvious reasons. The body corporate has no means by which to test the spirit to see if it is from God than by her own received modes of discipline and discernment. Otherwise, there is no way to know whether we are dealing with mere projection or genuine revelation. So ascesis and liturgy form us and tune us to receive the revelation, to encounter God and know that we can trust that encounter.[4]

An emphasis on the somatic nature of contemplation may, at first, seem contrary to the emphasis on its *spiritual* nature within the tradition. The fully "carnate" life of ancient Christians needed an emphasis on the incorporeal and psychic aspect of the contemplative life. On the contrary, our relatively extreme "excarnate" "social imaginary,"[5] demands an emphasis upon how such potentially psychological experiences of God made available to us through contemplation are not in addition to or in spite of the body, but made possible *through* bodily practices. They are not reducible to bodily practices, but, simultaneously, they are not possible for us—at least between the fall on the one hand and the eschaton on the other—without their mediation. Contemplation, for the Christian, is not the purely analytic conceptualizations of a Cartesian homunculus floating free of extension somewhere in the hypothalamus.

The modern Christian discomfort with an emphasis on the embodied nature of discipleship may be the symptom of a deeper problem discernable in the difference between the traditional body-soul anthropology of both the ancient world and Christian thought, and the modern philosophical dilemma of the mind-body problem.[6] Much of what modern thought would name *mental experience*, the ancients would have included as part of the experience of embodiment, and fallen embodiment at that. The modern mind-body dichotomy tends to lead Christians, especially in more colloquial contexts, to see the soul as consciousness and the body as that which lacks consciousness. This could not be further from the ancient body-soul anthropology of Christianity.

4. See David Fagerberg, *Liturgical Asceticism*. See especially his illuminative explication of the passions and *logismoi* with respect to the shared work of asceticism and liturgical participation.

5. See Charles Taylor, *A Secular Age*. Taylor coins the phrase "excarnate" to describe modern Cartesian disembodied constructions of the "self."

6. See Gerson, *Knowing Person*.

Consciousness, at least with regard to its particularity and individuation on the one hand and its tendency toward ego-projection on the other, are both epiphenomenon of embodiment after the fall. What we experience, when we experience anything, is the passions that only a body can experience. Thus, the soul transcends the body, as heaven does earth. The soul does not *experience* per se; the soul *forms* a human life in and as a human body. Paradoxically, because of the psychosomatic unity of human nature the soul may simultaneously be informed, reformed, or, sadly, deformed, by the course of the life of the body. This unfolding embodiment over time is exactly what makes repentance and, therefore, salvation, possible for human beings. And the formation of the soul by the body is what makes a sacramental economy not only fitting, but necessary to the nature of our somatic therapy.

Because of the confusion of the modern mind-body dichotomy with ancient body-soul anthropology, modern people of faith sometimes worry when there seem to be biological, neurological, or otherwise empirical accounts of things like religious or mystical experience, a sense of the presence of God, and other such transcendent realities.[7] Indeed, the scientists who present such findings often do so, or present them in such a way as to cause or exacerbate such religious anxiety. But if the soul is not locatable within the body and indeed, the body is the expression and manifestation of the soul in any given moment of time, then we should expect the whole body to be an expression of every physically expressible part or aspect of the soul—and that both corporally and corporately, for human embodiment is never merely individual. The mind, itself a property of the human, rational soul, does not exist in any one part of the body, even—as we late moderns are prone to think—in, say, the brain alone (*pace* Descartes' pituitary gland). It takes the whole body to think and choose as whole human beings.

Given the psychosomatic nature of being human, what else would mystical encounter, indeed, prophet knowledge itself, look like, then, from a purely methodologically empirical account? Must it not look like certain biological and neurological phenomenon in the brain and body? Physical accounts are only harmful to faith when extended beyond their empirical methodological strictures and made out to be exhaustive, reductive, or both. Empirical accounts of the religious and mystical can never be either

---

7. See Daniel Dennett, *Breaking the Spell*, for example.

exhaustive or reductive; they can, nevertheless, often prove helpful in many other ways.[8]

For example, consider that the hive aspect of being human and the loss of modern psychological individuality are related. According to recent psychological studies, the ability to achieve a kind of hive mind seems to be one of the very things that distinguishes us as human beings.[9] Chant, dance, ritual, liturgical behavior—all enable this hive mentality. This hive mentality suppresses the sense of individuation and thereby grants an experience of "oneness" with "the universe."[10] These may be some of the immanent level, but non-competitive empirical manifestations of the contemplation of God in general, and the sense of incorporation into the body of Christ in particular.

Thus, ascetical, and especially ritual, activity opens its participants to the contemplation of the mystery, and that through its very enactment. It is not so much that a corporate body enables contemplation, but that our shared contemplation through mimetic, somatic behavior grants disparate human bodies incorporation into a corporate body, into a shared cosmos. Mystical participation names a human gift from God of a hive behavior that enables a shared contemplation—and that, we hope, of the living God.

LITURGY AS RITUAL MYSTERY

The word *mystery* was already in use when deployed by the human authors of the new covenant Scriptures. "The root of our English word 'mystery' is

---

8. In another context, an analogous argument could be set forth for sensible epiphanies of the Lord.

9. See Haidt, *The Happiness Hypothesis*, 58. One of Haidt's central points is that the loss of human happiness under conditions of modernity is due in no small part to the loss of the opportunity to "live within the hive" for which we were built (or, "evolved," as his modern empirical language would have it). Haidt points to all the various means by which human beings achieve a genuine "corporate body" (my language) through this shared, or "hive" mind, especially citing ritual. Ritual action cannot be invented through a process of reasoning, it must invoke a bodily feeling through a community tradition that endorses and practices it—it must be part of the collective inheritance of a corporate body. Once the "hive mind" has shut down individuation, what people describe as "mystical experience" may arise. This common-place anthropological given, so lost on "excarnate" moderns, would have been assumed and simply *encountered*, by pre-modern (and still today many non-modern) Christians.

10. These are Haidt's words and would need some reworking in a directly Christian context.

a Greek verb, *muein*, which means to close the mouth."[11] Those who are initiated into the mystery are sworn to silence about something that cannot be talked about. But it could never really be a subject of conversation, for by its very nature it is not verbally comprehensible or exhaustible. The mystery comprehends the initiate, not the other way round. The initiate knows the mysteries by familiarity and intimacy, not by any kind of noetic, let alone discursive, comprehension. The mystery can be shown, witnessed, revealed, enacted, participated. It cannot be explained.[12]

An anthropological and historical analysis of the rise and function of the so-called mystery cults in the ancient Mediterranean Basin shows them to be largely Eastern religious traditions, which, in the face of increasing urbanization and cosmopolitanism, sought to preserve a given, diminishing agricultural cult by opening up the priestly franchise to a wider constituency—sometimes allowing any human being to receive initiation, even foreigners and slaves. The various mystery cults promised freedom from individual death, and that usually through some kind of apotheosis into the heavenly places. So what had been previously an entire cult system of civic and priestly liturgies become folded into a tighter liturgical whole.[13]

Ancient mystery cults were ritual behaviors. The mystery was enacted through ritual analogy. Thus, the real *mystery* of the cult was not so much the multiplicity of instances of individual human ritual initiations as the single cosmic initiation of the divine figure who falls or comes down from heaven (this is the case in many such myths, although some have the hero start out human), journeys to the underworld, returns again to the living, and is rewarded by being elevated among the gods—much like those myths of the ANE and Levant summarized above in Chapter One. The human *ritual* mystery serves only to inaugurate another human participant in this single cosmic reality.[14] Thus, *ritual* mystery and mystical *reality* correspond as analogues.

11. Hyde, *The Gift*, 366.

12. See Keller, "The Ritual Path" and Nancy Evans, "Diotoma and Demeter."

13. Liturgy, of course, encompasses many more ritual realities than simply those that describe mystery cults. But my focus in this chapter is on mysteries and their relationship to Christian liturgy. The summative nature of the development of mystery cults with respect to their previous local and agrarian setting renders them particularly appropriate summations of human religion at a general anthropological level. Remember, the Roman Catholic church, after Liturgical Renewal, even designates the divine service an initiation.

14. The above anthropological and historical summary depends upon the works

Anthropologically speaking, Christianity and rabbinic Judaism stand as sister religions inheriting a now lost temple cult in two different and now mutually incompatible streams. The starting point of difference between the two is the role of Jesus (or lack thereof) and the historical point of crisis being the destruction of the temple that he predicted. In light of this historical and anthropological take on mystery cults, Christianity, unlike rabbinic Judaism, may be understood in terms of the preservation of the Jerusalem temple cult (an "Eastern" religion), after the loss of the temple, by radically opening the franchise of the priesthood (via baptism) while simultaneously demanding (contrary to the pattern of all other ancient mystery cults) the same perfect exclusivity of devotion previously demanded by that lost temple.[15]

The priestly franchise of the Jerusalem temple-cult is now opened to all—not only those of Israel who are not of its priestly[16] lineage, but even to gentiles—through the new covenant ordination rituals of baptism.[17] The key difference between all previous iterations of this historical theme across mystery cults—of survival of rural cult through the opening of its franchise—is, of course, that Christianity forbids multiple associations and continued participation in anything other than the civic cultus of the

---

of Burkert and Eliade. See also McGowan, "Eucharist and Sacrifice," on the nature of Eucharistic sacrifice for the on-going connection to the Jerusalem temple cult.

15. While the temple still stood, the relationship of what would become Christianity to what would become Rabbinic Judaism was that of inner-Judaic rivalry and persecution. After the destruction of the temple, the Roman protection of Christians, as a kind of Jew, lifted, so pagan persecution began, leading, sadly, to the development of stronger polemical separation between the two Judaic groups.

16. I am grateful to Matthew Olver for alerting me to some objections high-church theologians may have to the above connection between baptism and Christian priestly ordination. As it is not immediately necessary to the flow of the argument, I can only address such worries briefly here in footnote. First of all, the Christian sacramental priesthood is primarily (historically and theologically) a *presbyterate*. Secondly, I am following Zizioulas's brilliant navigation between low-church functionalism with respect to holy orders and high-church ontological change. There is indeed an ontological change when a Christian takes one of the holy orders of the church. But what changes is the *body corporate*. The body is *ordered*—it receives the gift of holy order for the reasonable performance of the divine service (in all that the phrase "divine service" insinuates). All Christians are priests of the new covenant by virtue of their baptism. Some are called out to serve the kingdom of priests as bishops, presbyters, and deacons.

17. Despite problems, this seems to me to be Margaret Barker's key contribution to an historical analysis of the relationship of Jerusalem temple cult to the rituals of the developing church.

Jerusalem temple.[18] The Christian mystery initiates human being into an alternative and potentially universal hive, free of the damning competition and aggression between warring hives. In our historical case, these would be the city-states of the Mediterranean Basin. This is the very birth, in history, of *catholicity*. And the Christian ritual mysteries free us and incorporate us, paradoxically, by forcing the convert's renunciation of (at least the primacy of the claims made by) any other hitherto founded merely human hive.[19]

This key renunciation of the erstwhile human hive relationship gives Christianity its true power to turn the world upside down. Christianity's world-up-turning is *not* a continual *conceptual overturning* of goods basic to God's good creation—it is rather a return, through paradox, of and to these goods. God sustains and perfects nature by grace. Religion is natural to humanity, mystery religion an inherent part thereof.[20] In the ritual mysteries of the Christian faith, God makes use of intense ritual behavior and its ability to suppress the ego and to create a hive mentality in order, thereby, to generate a shared somatic contemplation, i.e., through baptism and the Eucharist we become the body of Christ.[21] Thus, by the paradox of

18. See Klawans, *Purity, Sacrifice*. Klawans notes the obvious continued temple worship of the church as reported, unapologetically, in the book of Acts. And this makes sense as it is exactly unauthorized initiation into the temple-cult that the Way offers to its adherents. Such unauthorized initiation would occur much to the chagrin of temple leadership. This may be what is going on when the temple sends representatives to investigate the baptism of John.

19. Thus we have Augustine's *City of God against the Pagans*.

20. Denial of such parallels of Christianity to general behaviors across human religion in general, and with the ancient mystery cults in particular, comes from, among other things, the fear of losing the uniqueness of Christ (and, thereby, the historic church), the historical concretion of the Christ-event (and church), or both. I wholeheartedly concur that Christianity and Judaism are unique. But this truth is an article of faith. I am not surprised when this article of faith goes unsupported by immanent theorizing. We do not need to fear commonalities of pattern. If we follow Lewis or Barfield on such matters, we should expect to see the logos at work throughout human ritual behavior if the realm of the heavenly has any reality whatsoever and if human beings have any contact thereto. If, the uppercase Logos of the Christian gospel is just a lowercase logos, and therefore a merely contingent or even projected thing, then Christian theology is in a lot of trouble. It is, in fact, a ridiculous illusion. Fortunately, for us, this is not in fact the case.

21. The ritual pattern of the Jerusalem temple enacted, among other things, the mystery of the creation of cosmos out of chaos in the ordination rituals for priests as well as the death and resurrection of the beloved Son in the Day of Atonement and other parallel rituals that correspond with the "twin" theme in Scripture.

our psychosomatic nature, a ritual initiation becomes for us our inauguration into the contemplation of God.

A brief note of qualification before going on: Christianity is not simply (the remains of) an ancient mystery cult with no remainder or difference. The other various mystery cults of the Greco-Roman world neither influenced nor caused Christianity (directly). Christianity as a human phenomenon has, nevertheless, an obvious social and cultural parallel development with the various mystery cults of the ancient Mediterranean with obvious analogical patterns. And, further, we should not be surprised to find that these represent concrete human manifestations of contact with transcendence. Christianity does not destroy but sustains and perfects such natural human manifestations of religious culture.

LITURGICAL THEOLOGY AS CONTEMPLATION OF CHRISTIAN MYSTERY

How does mystery and contemplation connect with Jesus' sacrifice and restart of the divine economy? Mystagogical initiation into and through Jesus Christ opens up our encounter with and recovery of the divine gift economy we lost. Jesus is the mystagogue; we are initiated into Jesus. In Jesus, we receive a liturgy and offer a sacrifice of thanksgiving. We are added to the mystery of God. So Jesus's sacrifice grounds our sacrifice and makes it acceptable to the Father. Jesus's *substitution* provides means and context for our *satisfactory* atonement. Satisfaction nests within that primordial substitution. Thus, all the various so-called theories of atonement represent discursive refractions of a single, liturgical whole.

Let us echo down the chain of manifestations: the pattern of theology is that of the divine life itself and God's economy of finite being. This pattern may manifest in the medium of our human intellect as contemplation and in our lives, somatically, as sanctification and, ritually, as liturgy and ascesis. Thus, while our minds become a medium of the divine pattern, paradoxically, as the soul is saved through the body in the Christian sacramental dispensation, the mind is therefore taken along for the ride, so to speak, in Christian sacramental initiation. The behavior of one level of reality becomes the pattern for the next level. The media provides the means for passing on the pattern. Contemplation is one of the media of our share in the economy. Therefore, when we take contemplation as the pattern, its medium for us as human beings is our embodied nature along the somatic continuum of corporate to corporal practices.

The soul is the form of the body and the body manifests the soul. Again, paradoxically, and fortunately, our bodily practices may in turn affect the state of our soul. Christian contemplation is not a practice in disembodiment. We do not contemplate ourselves separate from, over against, or in contrast to our bodies. Rather, we contemplate *in*, *as*, and *through* our bodies, through various behaviors and disciplines, e.g., ascesis and liturgy, appropriately corresponding to either the corporal or the corporate poles of our embodiment as human beings. They guide and initiate us into the contemplation of God. Our re-initiation into the divine economy grants our contemplative reception of the divine pattern as its psychic and noetic counterpart. Thus, liturgical theology is mystagogical contemplation.

The shared shape of the myths of the various mystery cults should be roughly recognizable to a modern Christian, for it is in general also the shape of the "myth" of Jesus Christ.[22] The Greco-Roman world certainly understood the religion of Judea and its peoples as Eastern. In the face of urbanization and cosmopolitanism, first-century Jews were faced with many problems for the traditional observance of their religion and found themselves divided between multiple and often contradictory approaches to the resolution to these problems. The early Christians opened the priestly franchise to any who would confess Jesus Lord and be baptized—even to the poor and enslaved. They promised freedom from the "second death" (Rev 2:11; 20:14) through theosis (2 Pet 1:4), rather than apotheosis. What had previously constituted an entire cultic system of a primarily agrarian people-group became folded into a tighter liturgical whole for its spread within multiple cosmopolitan environments.[23]

Further, and more importantly, the Christian mystery was not primarily a ritual activity for Christians, or even an initiation that made one Christian. The *mystical reality* is that of the Logos of God, his descent in incarnation as Jesus Christ, the paschal sacrifice he suffered, the descent among the dead, his vindication by his Father through resurrection, his ascension and return to the heavenly places wherein he was honored by

22. Lewis describes the importance of the discovery that perennial human myth does not occlude, but, if anything, corroborates the veracity of the Christian myth in his conversion narrative in *Surprised by Joy*. He also elaborates on this theme in his short essay, "Myth Became Fact."

23. See Meeks, *The First Urban Christians*. Christianity was largely an urban affair, just like the other mystery cults of the day.

sharing his Father's throne and rule. The Christian *ritual mystery* serves only to inaugurate other human participants into Christ's single, cosmic journey.

A pattern emerges. The Christian revelation witnesses an event: the divine economy of creation and its restart in the salvation offered by the sacrifice of Jesus Christ. Jesus restarts the tainted gift-exchange through his incarnate (re-)initiation into the Triune life of God. Jesus' behavior becomes an event the Christian witnesses. The Christian responds to this event with matching, mimetic behavior: primarily (willingness to undergo) martyrdom, or its near equivalent in a life of daily death to self. But, ritually, through mystagogical initiation into this cosmic mystery of the angelic gift economy, the ritual means of our share, and the ground and starting point of our life of divine service. "So mortals ate the bread of angels" (Ps 78:25). Our primary human medium engages our higher composition: mental, intellective, noetic contemplation. Contemplation is the noetic reception of the gift. But that enabled by somatic disciplines: the corporal through ascesis, the corporate through liturgy. Mystery is the somatic initiation into the gift economy. They mutually co-inhere. Thus, the liturgy is one of, and in many ways, the chief means by which we are inaugurated into Christ's mystery. Finally, and at a distant, analogical remove, we come to the part our human discourse plays as shareable noetic counterpart to the holistic salvation.

Human nature mixes things up a bit, both by our composite nature (body and soul) and by the conditions we find ourselves in after the fall. In terms of the economy received in the sacrifice of Jesus Christ, whatever self-sacrifice may mean for angels, it cannot mean what it does for us. For they are the pure intelligences; but we are a microcosm, a psychosomatic unity of body and soul. And although we are a "little lower than the angels," our relationship to the material order is fundamentally different from that of the angels. For angels do not create; but we sub-create[24] within the Creator in *imago Dei*. Liturgy for us as human beings (as opposed to, say, the angels) is a mystagogy, an initiation into the cosmos as a whole on the part of us as its microcosm. It turns out, what is revealed in our particular mystery, is that the cosmos is an economy, a gift economy and, therefore, a liturgy. Just as *anthropos* nests within the *cosmos*, even forming its microcosm, so too the Christian and his or her salvation nests within the sacrifice of Jesus Christ—again, even forming its epitome *in nucé.*

24. See Tolkien, *On Fairy Stories.*

Contemplation involves the body along its continuum as an apropos medium of divine revelation (reductive accounts not withstanding). Bodies cannot exist without flow of nourishment. The cycle of flow of a gift economy is the corporate analogue to the circulatory system in a given corporal body. Mystagogy is the initiation into and narration of that divine donation, going all the way back to its agrarian origins in the descent, consumption, and consummation of the deity. The ancient Christians named the ritual initiation into Christian faith *mystagogy*, by which they mean that which leads into the mystery. And this mystical behavior forms the ground of any discursive divine pattern recognition with respect to the Christian ritual mysteries. Our human nature nests in the economy described in the previous chapters; human being joins the corporate body of the incarnate God; in so doing, the *totus Christus* perfectly joins the trinitarian banquet and manifests it within the cosmos. Liturgical theology is the discourse that corresponds to this contemplative anthropology.

Insofar as the divine service on earth is not merely a human action, it is the ritual enactment and manifestation of this *theologia prima*. For *theologia prima* is this *Theos-Logos*, the incarnate God, suffering initiation into the cosmos for the sake of *anthropos*. "Great indeed, we confess, is the mystery of godliness: he was manifested in the flesh, vindicated by the Spirit, seen by angels, proclaimed among the nations, believed on in the world, taken up in glory" (1 Tim 3:16). We proclaim this mystery every time we recite the Creed. A given, concrete Christian liturgy becomes *theologia prima* only insofar as it is not merely human action but, through faith, and fidelity, it is swept up into and manifests this *theologia prima*: the mystery of the incarnation and paschal mystery of the Son of God. Liturgical theology, insofar as it is *theologia prima*, initiates Christians, through the cosmos, into the life of the Trinity that the Son suffers, this initiation, this divine mystagogy, in his incarnation as Jesus Christ. For the Christian ritual mystery incorporates the initiate into the body of Christ corporate, going where Christ has been, and returning with Christ on the Last Day. By him and with him and in him, the Christian returns to the peaceable kingdom of the Father before all worlds.

The Christian liturgy is a mystery—a mystical reality in the heavenly places, a ritual mystery for the faithful on earth. Mystery on our human plane is a ritual enactment and an initiation of the earthly into the heavenly. And these things are not two, but one. The ritual mystery shares the mystical reality. The mystical reality manifests, in the human corporate body, as

86

ritual mystery. Mystery names a dialogic between a ritual and the reality with which it resonates. Discursive reflection on the mystery therefore constantly alternates between the ritual mystery and its mystical reality. That is to say, between the divine pattern it seeks to discern and the ritual medium in which we discern it. The relationship of ritual mystery to mystical reality is not one of meaning, but of isomorphic homology across media and levels of scale. Reflection upon this connection of ritual mystery to mystical reality constitutes the key discursive task of liturgical theology.

Liturgical theology is our initiation into contemplation—a psychic and noetic reality—through and by means of a dynamic somatic process: the ritual mimesis of mystagogical initiations. What, again, is that Christian mystery? The Christian mystery has a discernible pattern, although it crosses many different levels of scale, nested continua, and media. So, it is the mystery of the relationship of persons within the Godhead before all worlds; it is the mystery of the relationship of God to creation, in general, where creation is a veil that simultaneously covers and reveals the divine nature; it is the mystery of the initiation of the Son of God through the sufferings of the cosmos, etc. Like a giant sheet thrown over an elephant, the contour lines reveal the erstwhile, unseen beast, so too our ritual patterns allow us to see as through a glass, darkly.

And these mysteries are all one, for they share the same transcendent pattern and source. The contemplative mystery is the ritual mystery as enacted at its cosmic level; it is the revelation of cosmos as ritual action. Our human ritual is our mimetic echo and resonant share in this cosmic contemplation of the Triune God. It is in fact identical with the cosmic liturgy, but at an analogical remove appropriate to our earthly, embodied human nature. The eschatic nature of liturgy is its completed state *sub specie aeternitatis*: when God will be all in all, and the cosmos itself becomes the elements of a great sacrament.

CONCLUSION

Liturgical theology is the contemplation of mystery,[25] where contemplation for us, as human beings, only ever exists in the medium of our human

---

25. Therefore, I intend by the phrase "contemplation of mystery," a double entendre where the preposition *of* is both instrumental and objective. That is to say, contemplation is simultaneously by means *of* mystery, and its subject matter is that of the reality resonating in the ritual action.

embodiment. The *theologia prima* of liturgical theology is that "initiation," through the cosmos, into the life of the Trinity, that the Son suffered, by virtue of being embodied, in the incarnation as Jesus Christ. For us, liturgical theology names the mystagogy—that is, the initiation into the ritual mysteries—that grants us a share in the mystery of Christ. Liturgical theology thus names somatic contemplation of the Christian mystery by means of its ritual enactment. At a further level of remove, liturgical theology names that discursive reflection on the nature of the mysteries themselves and the mystical reality to which they grant entrance.

Liturgical theology names the contemplation that comes as the result of initiation into the mystery of Christ. This contemplation is threefold. First, it names that "initiation," through the cosmos, into the life of the Trinity that the Son suffered in the incarnation of Jesus Christ. Next, at our human level of reality, it names the mystagogy that grants us a share in the mystery of the Christ. Liturgical theology thus names our somatic contemplation of the Christian mystery by means of its ritual enactment. Finally, at a further level of remove, liturgical theology names that discursive reflection on the nature of the mysteries themselves and the mystical reality to which they grant entrance.

The capacity for contemplation is the condition of the possibility of any revelation in general, and the revelation known as Scripture in particular. Ontologically, contemplation precedes the Holy Scriptures—the Scriptures themselves representing our collected and collective inheritance of trustworthy human contemplation of the divine. At our place in the timeline of unfolding history and fallen time, Scripture now norms Christian attempts at contemplation. Scripture has authority over any such attempts. But, ontologically, the Scriptures nest within our capacity for contemplation in the first place. The sacred Scriptures are the collected items of human literature authored by the Spirit (but including its human authors through non-competitive inspiration), thereby providing authoritative content to our human contemplation of God. In the next chapter, we turn to liturgical theology as the figural interpretation of Scripture.

Chapter 4

Liturgical Theology as Figural Interpretation

Theology is exegesis. Exegesis encounters the hermeneutical circle. The rule of faith provides a guiding narrative to the whole of which the various scriptures compose the parts. The exegete must receive some kind of means of initiation into this whole. So far we have explored how the liturgy is mystagogy that assumes the cosmic liturgy to be a divine economy. Our entry into this cosmic liturgy comes through martyrdom. Ritual entry, then, is martyrdom's enactment in the ritual mysteries. Knowledge of liturgy—that is, the cosmic and economic liturgy, its shape and various manifestations—grants a liturgical analogy to the rule of faith. This liturgical analogy empowers the imaginative processes of mystagogical catechesis and figuration.[1] Liturgical theology is thus the mystagogical entry into the hermeneutical circle that makes Christian sense of Scripture, that is to say, its figural reading.[2] This chapter will demonstrate that, among other things, liturgical theology names a kind of Christian interpretation theory.[3]

1. See de Lubac, *Medieval Exegesis* and Frei, *The Eclipse of Biblical Narrative,* and the many works they inspired.

2. De Lubac used the term *spiritual sense.* Frei and, more recently, Scott Hahn (see *Letter and Spirit*) say *typology.* I use the term *figuration,* following Augustine. It avoids the word *spirit,* with its inescapably multiple connotations in English. It simultaneously gathers up a broader meaning than typology alone, but nevertheless includes it. Many scholars who worry about typology would not worry about other traditional figurative senses, e.g., the tropological, which is used by every preacher to our own day.

3. See, for example, Behr's magisterial retelling of the development of theology and doctrine in the early church as primarily the development of, and attempt to remain faithful to, an inherited approach to the interpretation of Scripture (and that chiefly as the LXX) in his works, *The Way to Nicaea* and *The Nicene Faith.*

First, I explain that if theology is the interpretation of Scripture, then any definition of theology needs to be, if not primarily, at least substantially, hermeneutical in nature. Second, I look at how the cosmic divine economy, and even the divine life itself, is the most proper meaning of the word *liturgy*. I then turn to what the ancients called *mystagogical catechesis*, arguing that this catechesis forms the wider discourse that encompasses the figurative reading of Scripture. This allows me to assert that liturgical theology contemplates Scripture, when the narrative of the rule of faith summarizes a cosmic liturgy.

THEOLOGY AS EXEGESIS

⌈Hermeneutics and its circle maps human understanding to the relationship between parts and wholes. In short, parts make sense within a whole. The whole is understood by comprehending the parts. Entry into the circle is ⌊made possible only with at least an initial grasp of the whole. Liturgical theology treats the liturgy as the whole that grants comprehension.[4] By that, I mean the cosmic liturgy of the divine economy. The parts discerned are themselves often concrete liturgies, but also include the Christian life, call, and gospel. This is to say that liturgical theology interprets Scripture.

Recall the foundational hermeneutics of Augustine's *de doctrina Christiana*.[5] Augustine identifies a fundamental difference between signs and things. All signs are things, but not all things are signs. Within this sign-to-thing relationship, Augustine relates the parts of Scripture to the whole of Scripture. The initial grasp of Scripture comes through the rule of faith, and rule of faith as summarized by Christ in his person, and verbally in the summation of the law. But the Scriptures themselves are a part of God's created reality as a whole. Entry into reality as a whole comes only through the imitation of the saints. Under this hermeneutic, figuration occurs when the context of the canonical Scriptures as a whole is construed to be the divine economy. In any point of human history the saints have contemplative access to the divine economy. And accordingly, any Christian has a similar access through the imitation of the saints.

Recall the geometrical relationship of squares to rectangles discussed in the introduction. This relationship provides an excellent analogy for

4. See Zimmerman's excellent work with this regard in her book on Ricoeur, *Liturgy as Language*, and in her summary of this topic, *Liturgy and Hermeneutics*.

5. See Augustine, *De Doctrina Christiana*.

hermeneutics. Not all rectangles are squares, but all squares are rectangles. Modern hermeneutics rediscovered that human being recognizes patterns in behavior and that such recognition is itself behavior.[6] Understanding itself is an action. Squares are rectangles, but not all rectangles are squares. I take the rectangle-to-square distinction to be a contemporary restatement of Augustine's point about things and signs. All signs are things, but not all things are signs. All discourse is behavior, but not all behavior is discursive.[7] Not all action is understanding, but understanding is an action. Not all patterns are recognition, but all recognition is a pattern.

Are actions meaningless until understood? Not necessarily. Is understanding impotent until enacted? By definition.[8] Meaning proceeds from act, and speech and ritual are both actions. Action is primary. It is the outward correlate of the will. This is why Christianity ultimately did not become a gnostic cult. It is love (which, of course, requires and generates knowledge), and not knowledge (alone) that saves.

So, we may ask, which is foundational, act or understanding? One of the primary gifts of liturgical theology is the reassertion of this hermeneutical claim of a foundational ontology of action over understanding, event over meaning.[9] This reassertion of the primacy of behavior is neither an historical nor a procedural claim, nor is it in competition with such claims. Recognizing the primacy of behavior is a categorical claim about human nature made from a Christian theological and modern cultural anthropological point of view.

But our picture of theology would not be complete without also recalling that, unlike almost every other kind of human discourse or science, theology is about allowing for and even expecting, transcendent causality and transcendent accounts of reality. Now we can combine the geometrical analogy of squares and rectangles to human science, even human nature, with the point that theology looks for transcendent patterns. The result

6. So, for example, Ricoeur's event and understanding and Gadamer's play and being "called up short," etc.

7. See discussion above in the Introduction.

8. This understanding of the need for enactment to render understanding is still compatible with a strictly Thomistic (and Aristotelian) account of the centrality of contemplation when we construe contemplation as the chief human goal or act. Even if contemplation has no immediate this-worldly concretion, it is nevertheless only achieved through an act of the will.

9. This functional ontology is the real importance behind the claim that liturgy is *theologia prima*, introduced by Kavanagh in *On Liturgical Theology*.

delivers a solid working definition of what Christians understand theology to be. Christian theology searches for the highest humanly possible level of pattern recognition: transcendent, even divine, pattern recognition.

When we combine this hermeneutical insight with the theological goal of discerning transcendent patterns, we discover the chief logic of theology: analogy. Transcendent patterns are recognizable through immanent manifestations. Assuming God's non-competitive transcendence, theology regains the paradox wherein divine initiative does not destroy but entails, enables, empowers, renders possible and real, human participation in transcendence, even divinity, without a reduction of such transcendence to mere human immanence. Non-competitive participation retains the discrete otherness of creatures within the Creator. Such non-competitive participation allows human rites to become mysteries, human persons to become saints, and even human language itself to become a conduit of the gift of theology, contemplation.

The rule of faith provides theology's chief guiding analogy. The rule of faith summarizes the divine economy, providing an initial grasp of that whole in which we find Scripture. Liturgical theology takes the rule of faith as the summary of a liturgy. The chief analogy for liturgical theology is that the whole is analogous to a ritual mystery. *Theology* means "exegesis," contemplative engagement with Scripture. Now the chief Christian interpretation of Scripture is divine service itself. Thus, liturgical theology applies its analogy to Scripture, and only after that, to concrete human enactments of the ritual mysteries. In this sense, then, the ritual mysteries may become *theologia prima*. A given, concrete Christian liturgy becomes *theologia prima* only insofar as it is not merely a human interpretation of Scripture, but an incarnation of the Word of God. What, then, is the liturgy of scriptural interpretation?

LITURGY AS MYSTAGOGY

The *liturgy* of liturgical theology comprises not so much concrete human ritual acts on earth as it does a construal of the divine economy as an act of worship in the heavenly places. Liturgical theology nevertheless reflects on earthly human worship. When it does so, however, it reflects on human worship as participating in and manifesting the divine economy, construed under the analogy of a cosmic formal act of worship, liturgy. Theologically speaking, then, human rites are liturgy only insofar as they manifest this fundamental reality, this fundamental divine service, this fundamental liturgy.

Recent scholarship on the Old Testament and ancient Israelite worship has discerned a kind of weft holding together the various threads of warp that make up the elaborate tapestry of the old covenant canon.[10] Let us call this weft the *temple-mythos*. By *temple-mythos*, I intend that shared transcendent cosmology assumed across the old (and new) covenant Scriptures. The word *myth* is not pejorative. *Myth* here means human narrative about transcendent reality or realities. This kind of myth is not simply pagan or heathen "lies." A serious look at the ancient Israelite temple-mythos does not entail a reduction of Judaism or our own Judaic inheritance as Christians to such (in the main unhelpful) construals of non-biblical religion.

The term *temple-mythos* avoids other infelicitous terms. For example, the term *biblical worldview* conjures up representational reductionism, privileging cognition over practice. *Apocalyptic* or *apocalypticism* connotes both more and less than I intend—more, because of contemporary connotations, less because *apocalyptic* represents only one kind of literature that shares a modus operandi with other types of literature within the old covenant canon (indeed, within ancient Mediterranean culture in general). The old contrast between apocalyptic and oracular prophecy breaks down when it becomes clear that these are different literary types demanded by historical exigencies, rather than products of different ritual-mythological practices. *Apocalyptic* itself is a kind of disenfranchised wisdom literature: what those who possess wisdom see when they are in exile, rather than in the court of the king.[11] The ritual actions described in the old covenant form the ritual counterparts to this shared cosmology. The foundational narratives of Genesis may be read as the discursive counterparts to these very rituals. The temple-mythos also overcomes the discursive priority implied in worldview language that might overturn the dynamic dialectic that actually holds between ritual and myth. The phrase *temple-mythos* expresses the ritual-narrative patterns that these various forms of literature and behavior share.

The temple-mythos operates in a cosmos that is (a service of) worship. What cosmos is, that is to say "beautiful order," is a divine service before its Creator. The service *is* the cosmos: its liturgy renders cosmos out of chaos. This cosmic liturgy has a cosmic *ordo*, and that ordo is what the Christian

10. Again, see especially the works of both Barker and Levenson.

11. Levenson, *Creation,* 32.

tradition calls the *economy*. Ritual mysteries do not accidentally manifest a reality altogether foreign to them. It is fitting that a (human) ritual act of worship should manifest the economy, because the economy itself is an act of organized (if celestial) worship.

Much of the recent temple-mythos literature available seemed at first to me, as a Christian theologian, to assume a far too *in illo tempore* style. I struggled with what this might mean. If the Lord separates the waters in the heavenly places to render cosmos out of chaos, does that turn Jesus into another one, albeit important, among many historical manifestations of an eternal truth? In other words, I felt the weight of the historical uniqueness of Jesus. I had not yet reversed the analogy and crossed over into anagogy.[12]

In a Christian theological context, Jesus (his incarnation, life, teaching, and paschal mystery) *is* the cosmic liturgy, the physical touch-down, the entry or manifestation, the parousia of the Lord, the Son of the Most High God, in his work as high priest over the cosmic liturgy. For the priest must come to the altar (earth) in order to offer the appointed sacrifice (himself). This Christian theological reading of the temple-mythos leads, therefore, to a theological—and in this case, economic—definition of liturgy. A theological take on the temple-mythos connects the rites of the Old and New Testaments, opening new ground for liturgical theological contemplation.

Liturgical theology not only makes an analogy from what (anthropologists and historians agree that) we call *liturgy* for the life and economy of God, it also *reverses* the analogy. Liturgical theology is anagogy. The theological meaning is the primary Christian meaning of *liturgy*.[13] What we call liturgy on earth is a ritual participation in this cosmic hymn of praise. The economy is the liturgy: the work of the Son of God, our great high priest, on behalf of the people of God. Liturgical theology needs such a theological definition of liturgy, one that makes God the actor and God's mighty deeds the main action, in order to approach the task *theologically*, rather than as thoughtful religious gloss on history or historical (or sociological) study. The rule of faith summarizes a liturgy. Such an exegetical and scriptural approach was assumed rather than stated by the ancient producers of the earliest commentaries on the Christian mysteries: mystagogical catechesis.

12. See my discussion of anagogy and Denys in the Introduction.

13. With that as the case, then liturgical theology can make the following kinds of claims: the life of God is a kind of liturgy unto itself, the divine economy is a liturgy, the incarnation is *the* liturgy of atonement, theosis is human participation in Christ's cosmic liturgy, our participation in divine service, etc.

MYSTAGOGICAL CATECHESIS

Recall that ritual initiation into the Christian faith is mystagogy, that which leads into the mystery. This mystical behavior forms the ground of discursive divine pattern recognition with respect to the Christian ritual mysteries. Discourse about the mysteries the ancient Christians called mystagogical catechesis. Mystagogical catechesis names that discourse that identifies the ritual mysteries as manifestations of, and initiations into, the mystery of the divine economy itself. Scholarship on the nature of patristic mystagogical lectures[14] has in general drawn the following analogy: mystagogical catechesis is to the sacraments as figuration is to Scripture.

If, however, we remember our squares and rectangles, then mystagogy must name the ground of both catechetical lectures concerning mystagogy and the figurative reading of Scripture. If liturgy is the behavior (rectangle) and Scripture is its native discourse (square), then discourse *about* the liturgy—namely, mystagogical catechesis—grounds the discourse that engages those Scriptures read *within* liturgy (which is just to say the figurative reading of Scripture). In other words, figuration names the mystagogical reading of Scripture. When we read the Scriptures figuratively, we read them with the assumption that they, like Christian rites, manifest realities that infinitely exceed them, yet nevertheless behave in discernible and imitable patterns. Mystagogy and figuration are one, because the Scriptures are a part of the divine service, just as discourse is a part of human behavior. Thus, liturgical theology as figural interpretation of Scripture finds its chief instance in that interpretation of Scripture we call the divine service—the enactment of Scripture in the life of Christ, the life of the saint, in the ritual mimesis of the Christian mysteries.

There are differing and even seemingly incompatible mystagogical treatises that survive. We cannot give a unified historical account of what mystagogical catechesis was, is, or should be.[15] This is because of the nature of mystagogy itself. The goal of catechetical lectures on mystagogy is the contemplation of things that, from beyond human historical experience (much less human historiography), give human life and history meaning

---

14. See Mazza, *Mystagogy*. Also, Scott Hahn has shown the formal and material unity of mystagogy, figuration, and a patristic approach to the divine economy. My point complements his, but my point is more directly theological: the divine economy *is the liturgy*, at least, it is the liturgy that forms the adjective in the phrase "liturgical theology," and that just exactly because it is theological.

15. Mazza, *Mystagogy*, 165.

and transcend it (and in the case of the Triune God, infinitely so). We can, however, give a unified—or, at least, general or unifying—account of what mystagogical catechesis is, theologically considered. Theologically, mystagogical catechesis names that discourse that identifies the ritual mysteries as manifestations of, and initiations into, the mystery of the divine economy itself.

Given such a theological definition, it makes sense that there could never be a single unifying historical instance of mystagogical catechesis. The historical diversity should be expected due to its shared theological reality. Allowing for mutual and even seemingly incompatible contemplations is a sign that what we are engaging in is catholic. You cannot simultaneously perform the anaphora of St. John Chrysostom and the Roman Canon of the Mass. That does not make them incompatible, it makes them catholic.

Mystagogical catechesis and figuration are one, then, because the Scriptures are a part of the divine service. For when we contemplate the divine life and economy as the most proper meaning of the word *liturgy*, what the tradition calls figuration and mystagogical catechesis represent two modes of discourse about the same theological reality. Mystagogical catechesis is the wider discourse, encompassing the figurative reading of Scripture. Figuration performs mystagogy on Scripture. Thus, liturgical theology forms an essential part of a post-critical retrieval of both mystagogy and figuration.

LITURGICAL THEOLOGY AS FIGURAL EXEGESIS

Liturgical theology names a retrieval of ancient mystagogical catechesis and the figural interpretation it assumed and supported.[16] Liturgical theology, as mystagogical catechesis before it, is the contemplation of the divine life and economy, and even the cosmos itself, as a liturgy, indeed, as liturgy. Liturgical theology names a retrieval of the ancient theological, economic, and cosmological background, what I have been calling the temple-mythos, which manifested the twin ancient discourses of catechetical mystagogy and figuration.

Theology names faithful Christian exegesis of Scripture, not interpretation of ritual per se. An adjective in front of the word *theology* gives an

16. Mazza, *Mystagogy*, xii. Here, Mazza calls mystagogy an ancient "liturgical theology."

analogical construal of the rule of faith, which serves as the entry point of a given Christian contemplation of sacred text. In our case, then, liturgical theology must necessarily be a kind of "interpretation theory."[17] The "liturgy" of liturgical theology is the divine life and economy presented, biblically, as a temple-mythos. This temple-mythos is, then, the "whole" of our liturgical theological hermeneutical circle.

Figuration occurs when Christians construe the context of the canonical Scriptures as a whole to be the divine economy—accessible through contemplation to the body of Christ (both corporate in the form of catholic churches and corporeal in the multitude of the saints) in any point of earthly history. Mystagogical catechesis unfolds when Christians understand the ritual mysteries to manifest and initiate the Christian into the mystery of this divine economy. In both cases, the realization that the divine economy *is* the divine liturgy retrieves figuration and mystagogy, for God's temple (house) is the cosmos as a whole.[18]

Liturgical theology names and contemplates the whole *as liturgy* in order to expound both rite, on the one hand (mystagogical catechesis), and Scripture, on the other (figuration), as parts of the one reality they manifest: the divine service of Jesus Christ. Liturgical theology articulates the ritual pattern, the enacted figure that *is* the ritual we call the service of the Word. The ritual proclamation of Holy Scriptures is liturgical theology, where *liturgy* is the service of the Word and *theology* is the Word of the Lord—incarnate in human literature.

Reading the rule of faith as a narrative summary of a cosmic liturgy brings together traditional readings of the mysteries, the canon as Scripture, and critical scholarship on the ancient temple-mythos. Post-criticism assumes the importance of historical readings without criticism's reductionism. In this case, a post-critical approach reintegrates the kind of historical construction that uncovers a temple-mythos in the ancient Levant with traditional readings of the canon by allowing for the possibility that the transcendent realities discerned within the mythos, and the Scriptures and rites believed to place us in contact with them, may in fact be real, and not (human) projections.

---

17. Ibid., 135.

18. Even if this is not the only or exclusive way to construe the divine economy (and, of course, it is not), it is still at least sound and, I would argue, a central way of doing so, due to the centrality of the love of God in worship, corporate worship, and liturgical worship in Scripture and the tradition.

Liturgical theology is also that discourse that assumes the mystery as the whole of the hermeneutical circle. The hermeneutical circle of liturgical theology is that of concrete sacred texts and ritual behavior (parts) to cosmic divine service (whole) and back, linked by discerning webs of overlapping transcendent, participatory causality. The way we enter this hermeneutical circle is through participation in the mysteries themselves, that is to say, through mystagogy, proper, with the faith that they manifest the divine economy. Figural interpretation fits within a mystagogical economy, where initiation, somatic initiation in the mystery of Christ inaugurates our entry into what is most real. It is fitting that a ritual act of worship would manifest the economy if the economy itself is an act of organized, if celestial, worship.

Let us now echo down the chain of manifestations. Recall that the noetic counterpart to theosis in general is the gift of contemplation in particular. A key medium of that contemplation is liturgy. We encounter God in contemplative union. Our temporal embodiment and fallen condemnation to death leads to another behavior: recording. We write down and accumulate the collective contemplations of the body of the faithful. These writings are performed at the liturgy. Over time, a material cultural feedback loop develops as these contemplations of the tradition are accumulated and collected into an authoritative canon of Holy Scripture. This canon, in turn, becomes normative for future contemplation within the tradition. Behavior then leads discourse, where we extend forward the collected and now authoritative contemplations of the tradition through their ongoing interpretation: exegesis into the lives of saints, liturgical performance, and contemplative union.

The hermeneutical circle of liturgical theology is not, therefore, that of the particulars of history or sociology to their broader historical or sociological context and back again. For this hermeneutical circle only discerns chains of immanent causal links—be it chronological or social. Liturgical theology contemplates Scripture assuming that, because both the Scriptures and the mysteries participate in the realities of heaven, and because the native context of scriptural contemplation is that of the ritual mysteries, being open to the realities with which the mysteries place us in contact will help us to elucidate the meaning of the Scriptures, and vice versa.

Now, we may be "pulled up short"[19] by many things: a passage of Scripture about rites[20] or a passage of Scripture not seemingly about ritual,[21] or even (seemingly) anti-ritual.[22] We are caught up short by concrete acts of Christian liturgy here on earth, or discovered or rediscovered historical liturgical texts, long lost to any living Christian tradition.[23] Even so, we return to Scripture for insight.[24] Either way, what completes the circle is the divine liturgy of the heavenly places, the liturgy that is the life of God: the Holy Trinity (Chapter One),[25] and the cosmic liturgy of the paschal mystery (Chapter Two). This final point, at least, we find attested in the book of Hebrews.

SACRIFICE AND FIGURATION

The new covenant Scriptures do not have an entire book within them dedicated to either the kingship or prophetic office of Jesus. The new covenant Scriptures do, however, possess within them a book that is dedicated to an exposition of Jesus as priest and victim.[26] The author of the book of

19. This is Gadamer's phrase for what initiates the need for interpretation, in *Truth and Method*, 280.

20. For instance, the Day of Atonement, or the sacrifice of the first-born to Molech.

21. Or the way in which the Eden story is actually about a primordial temple.

22. Or the way in which passages in the oracular prophets seem to denigrate sacrifice and ritual worship all together. If liturgy is so central, how do we make sense of these? The first two chapters address this question in part.

23. For instance, both concrete and living liturgical traditions and "found" liturgies from ancient texts. Theologically speaking, however, living liturgies must take precedence over discoveries.

24. Consider how the solution to the problem of the *Didache*'s "prayer of consecration" was found in reading the so-called "words of institution" in Scripture as an ordo, rather than a consecratory formula. A careful reading of the Scriptures themselves empowered a movement away from "prayers of consecration," and "consecratory formulae" back to Eucharistic Prayers.

25. Liturgical theology does not, therefore, meditate upon concrete Christian ritual per se, any more than theology is a meditation on concrete Christian individuals. It is an exercise in noticing transcendent patterns that these concrete individual realities (are able to) share in and manifest.

26. I am alluding here to the classical threefold office, which, although not necessarily a biblical classification, is nevertheless foundational in Christian thought. Perhaps the new covenant Scriptures demanded a book like that of Hebrews exactly because Jesus was not an earthly priest in Herod's temple. Perhaps the point needed driving home more than that of the other two offices. That said, Hebrews's emphasis on Jesus' priesthood

Hebrews interprets the life, the office, and especially the paschal mystery of Jesus to be the Day of Atonement (discussed previously in Chapter Two), and that construed, consistently, as cosmic in nature and scope.[27]

The author of Hebrews carefully sets up this argument. First, the author makes clear that Jesus is qualified to be priest by virtue of a different order, the order of Melchizedek. Hebrews then asserts that Jesus, as sinless, need not atone for himself or his family. The high priest puts on ritual clothing, the Son puts on flesh: "a body you have prepared for me" (Heb 10:5, quoting Ps 40:6–8). Jesus puts on the Divine Name, being made a Son through obedience. Animals are substitutes. The high priest, as the Lord's ritual persona, cannot literally immolate himself and complete the ritual. But Jesus can and does. One cannot simultaneously send out and immolate the same goat. But Jesus is both scapegoat and Lord. And the author of Hebrews adjures his first-century Christian audience to die with Jesus "outside the city" (Heb 13:12).[28] In ascension, Jesus enters the most holy place not "made by human hands" (Heb 9:24), and begins the act of cosmic atonement, cleansing the temple that is the cosmos. As the high priest emerges from the temple to bless the people, so Jesus "will appear a second time, not to deal with sin, but to save those who are eagerly waiting for him" (Heb 9:28). The return of Christ closes the cosmic ritual action; we find ourselves in a time distended between unified cosmic ritual actions.

"Of these things we cannot now speak in detail" (Heb 9:5), but I hope to follow up with further research. Still, if the "myth" enacted in the ritual of the Day of Atonement is cosmic in scope and ramification, then the book of Hebrews interprets Jesus as that myth incarnate. If we turn from historical reconstruction to the task of theology, allowing transcendent causality, then a significant shift in perspective occurs. Jesus Christ presides over the cosmic liturgy, or, rather, the liturgy that *renders* cosmos, that *is* cosmos. In his earthly sojourn, the Lord impresses this ritual shape, or ordo, upon earth and history as Jesus's life, teachings, and paschal mystery.

---

could also be interpreted as an emphasis on the ancient Israelite tradition of sacral kingship. See the works of Margaret Barker.

27. See Barker, *Temple Themes*.

28. Although not referred to explicitly in the Book of Hebrews, the scapegoat is central to the rite of the Day of Atonement, which is the key ritual focus of the book. I take, therefore, the reference to Jesus' dying "outside the city" as a double entendre on both the sacrifices burnt outside the camp and the scapegoat driven away from the camp.

Now, in Christ, we know that *Endzeit gleicht urzeit.*[29] The economy of cosmos is the protological liturgy. The economy of cosmos is the liturgy of the eschaton. The cosmic liturgy, *in illo tempore*, manifests temporally in Christ and perennially in the ritual mysteries. The liturgy is this divine service, that is to say, the life, ministry, and paschal mystery of Jesus Christ and its local and repeated manifestations in every holy Christian body, at every sacred feast. All Christian liturgy is one. The differences are those of nested continua, their varying levels of scale, and their transfer across given media and their relative condition (fallen or not). But the fundamental pattern is the same.

If Christian theology uses anthropological reductions of sacrifice uncritically, it runs the danger of making it sound as though ancient Jews or ancient Israel somehow fell short of God's will by obeying the commandments given them by that very God. The scapegoat becomes part of the problem rather than God's revealed solution. The straightforward supersessionism, and perhaps subtle anti-Semitism, in such positions needs to be named.

The traditional Christian account actually avoids such supersessionism by seeing the system of sacrificial substitution as witness on one side of the paschal mystery to that which the Holy Eucharist participates in on this side of the mystery. Both old and new covenants express, on different sides of human time, the *same* divine reality and mode of God's relating to human beings: covenant and sacrifice. There is only one divine economy, one mystical reality. The heavenly pattern, the divine economy, has not changed. The earthly manifestation—the medium in which the pattern manifests—this alone has changed. The difference between the old and new covenant therefore is not that of lesser to greater, or immature to more mature, but of *anticipation* to *recollection* of the Gift. Only insofar as recollection seems "better" than anticipation can we say the new "abolishes" the old. I take this to be the meaning of such language in the book of Hebrews when the author calls Christ the "mediator of a *better* covenant" (Heb 8:6, emphasis mine).[30]

---

29. Levenson, *Creation*, 27.

30. Klawans still attributes supersessionism to the book of Hebrews. I believe this is mistaken. His otherwise excellent retrieval of ancient Hebrew sacrifice and ancient Christian continuation and extension of the same still fails to see the way in which the book of Hebrews fits into the general pattern he has discerned.

The old ecclesial term of *shadow* can itself also be read in supersessionist ways.[31] I want to avoid that as well. The relationship of old rites to the new is a relationship of shadow to reality only so long as we understand shadow in the ancient figurative sense of that which *clearly shows* the shape of the thing for which it shadows, and by it allows us to recognize it when we turn from the shadow to that which casts it.[32] We know a tree is behind us because it casts a clear and distinctly recognizable shadow upon the ground. The shadow of a tree is an inherent part of the reality, *tree*. The rites, sacrifices, and purity codes of the old covenant are the clear and articulate shadow cast by the paschal mystery when the light of the consummation shines on that part of the history of the people of God that falls prior to the incarnation of the Son of God. Such a vision honors the Old Testament *as Christian Scripture*, which is necessary in order to avoid supersession, while avoiding an interpretation of the old covenant as a revelation distinct from that of Christ, a position unacceptable to traditional Christian practice, and far too amenable to anti-Semitic thinking.

Just as the human environment is suffused with divinity, so too, in incarnation, the divine Logos' environment now suffuses, and is suffused with, humanity, even cosmos. Jesus' divine-human environment is suffused with the presence of saints (e.g., the transfiguration [Matt 17:1–8; Mark 9:2–8; Luke 9:28–36]). But, moreover, "Do you think that I cannot appeal to my Father, and he will at once send me more than twelve legions of angels?" (Matt 26:53), Jesus asks his disciples. For his environment includes the very council of the 'elohim. But he must not abrogate his priestly role—he must fulfill the liturgy.

The heavenly places, although not eternal in the sense of the divine nature, nevertheless enjoy the sempiternity of bodiless motion.[33] The con-

31. I find this to be the case even with a great writer like Congar, or his peer, de Lubac. The language of shadow can be the language of anticipatory articulation, or it can be used as the language of absence to presence. I want the former and to avoid the latter.

32. The word *shadow* (*skia*), "can be used spatially to distinguish heavenly reality from its earthly shadow and temporally to distinguish a present shadow from a future reality[;] . . . shadows retain the shape of the object that casts them and can therefore help one discern what is real." Craig R. Koester, "Hebrews," *The Anchor Bible*, 377.

33. See Aquinas's account of angelic incorruptibility, *ST* I, Q. 50. Aquinas here (as in many other areas) represents the culmination of a long debate within the tradition concerning whether or not angels are embodied but with purer, rarefied, ethereal bodies, or, whether they are bodiless pure intelligences. The tradition has tended now to go with Aquinas's interpretation of angels as pure intelligences. Nevertheless, because the word was still out on this issue for quite some time, reading the older ethereal bodies

nection between the texts is, therefore, heavenly in the sense of the angelic, the cosmic, the aveternal. The connection is mediated by the key location of the transfer of patterns across such nested continua in the gift we know of as ritual. This gives a rich theological context for non-reductive figurative reading of the relationship of Jesus, Jesus' sacrifice, and various old covenant texts, both ritual and narrative. Again, reductive readings either (in some pre-critical cases) make old covenant pericopes merely types, or shadows, in the sense of inferiority, or (in the case of reductive anthropology) lack ontological richness or contact with transcendence. The connection across the texts is neither mere projection nor a paranormal extrasensory perception. For the connection is in the heavenly places, mediated or "conducted" via ritual and the liturgical. We thus avoid shades and projections. Figuration makes no sense, and may be, in fact, dangerous, outside of mystagogy. In conclusion, let me give one more scriptural example.

LITURGICAL FIGURATION

"Your Father Abraham rejoiced to see my day: and he saw it, and was glad" (John 8:56 NASB). How did Abraham see the day? In the same way we do under conditions of the new covenant: through ritual mystery, through analogical liturgical enactment. The rites of the new covenant recall, in the main; Abraham anticipates, in the main. Both participate, equally and fully. The sacrifice of Isaac ritually enacts the paschal mystery before the Mosaic covenant will provide a temple-sacrificial system of substitution to do so for the corporate body of Israel. Thus, the author of Hebrews can straightforwardly assert that Abraham did receive Isaac back from the dead, through resurrection (Heb 11:17–19), *as in a mystery*: ritual enactment.[34]

All this is possible because, and only because, "before Abraham was, I am" (John 8:56). The Gospels reveal the earthly, tragic, bungled trial and torturous death of Jesus of Nazareth together with his resurrection on the third day, in a mystery, as the sacrifice of the incarnate God, the great

---

angelology analogically into the now more traditional bodiless intelligences angelology should prove an illuminating project.

34. Indeed, this must be the case or we fall into supersession—the divorcing of the testimonies of each covenant to each other. The recognition of patterns across historical instance grounds all Christian exegesis, especially that of the Scripture first recognized by the church, what we now call the Old Testament. Thus, the Christian tradition of biblical exegesis has always included figuration even if with varying degrees of focus and intensity.

cosmic liturgy over which the Lord himself presides: "Can you draw up Leviathan with a hook?" The Lord can, and does so in conquering chaos and death through paschal mystery. And if it is cosmic, then Abraham can connect with it as in a mystery, like any other ritual analogical translation of patterns across nested continua of God's created reality. Abraham "sees" Jesus without need of extrasensory perception such as precognition because the rite participates in the reality itself, apocalyptically, whether Abraham is noetically aware of it fully, or not. As with all liturgical participants before and after him, Abraham knows that which the ritual conveys, as in a mystery, ontically, regardless of cognitive association or its relative depth. And this is good news for us as well, for just as father Abraham of old we see as in a glass, darkly.

Before concluding, it is fair for me to note that my audience and I are both trained up and formed in critical approaches to Scripture under the paradigm of modern secular nominalism. So in all fairness I ought to make plain what I am saying here and what I am not. I am not asserting such interpretations as (modern) historical (or, rather, historicizing) readings. I am not asserting these readings as any kind of assessment of the psychological state of Abraham, Isaac, or any other person accounted for in Scripture. (We must hope that psychological state is not a condition of liturgical participation; for if it were, as none of us fully grasp what we are doing when we make so bold as to come before the throne of grace in divine service, we would all find ourselves disqualified. Thankfully, God's mercy endures forever.) I am asserting this as an appropriate figure, where *figure* is construed as a theological and not merely literary reality. Such figures manifest a theological reading of the text, taking as given that the sacrifice of Jesus' Christ is the cosmic liturgy as manifested in the earthly places and transgresses the bounds of human history.

CONCLUSION

Liturgy is mystagogy and mystagogy assumes the divine economy is a cosmic liturgy. Theology is exegesis and demands some kind of hermeneutical circle and some means by which we may be initiated into it. Thus, among other things, liturgical theology names a kind of Christian interpretation theory. Liturgical theology provides the mystagogical entry into the hermeneutical circle that makes Christian sense of Scripture, that is to say, its figural reading. Entry is found in martyrdom, anticipated through its enactment in the ritual mysteries. Knowledge of liturgy—that is, the cosmic and economic liturgy, its shape and various manifestations—grants a liturgical approach to the rule of faith for the imaginative processes of mystagogical catechesis and figuration. If our figuration as Christians is not mere projection, but takes some purchase upon reality, then liturgical theology demands a kind of Christian metaphysical realism. In the next chapter, we turn to liturgical theology as apocalyptic realism.

Conclusion

Liturgical Theology as Apocalyptic Realism

An apocalyptic realism has become the cumulative implication of our economic anagogy, where liturgy is a ritual apocalypse and theology is a kind of Christian metaphysical realism. Theology as transcendent pattern recognition demands realism if it is to acknowledge that the patterns it recognizes are not mere projection, nor the accumulated detritus of an abstract history of ideas. Liturgy is a ritual apocalypse if it is the expression of genuine contact with transcendence, rather than merely an atomized instance of habitual behavior disconnected from every other discrete instance. Liturgical theology is an apocalyptic realism.

Each of the previous chapters suggested an anagogical interpretation of liturgy. We encounter God and the gift of creation. The behavior is worship of the Creator, an orderly worship that itself dynamically establishes order. The discourse is the Holy Scriptures and our contemplation thereof. Created economies, liturgies, form mere analogues to the liturgy of the divine economy. Human liturgical economics form an analogy to the cosmic economy, the angelic liturgy. Ritual sacrifice is analogous to the sacrifice of Jesus Christ. Ritual initiation is analogous to Jesus Christ's incarnation and paschal mystery. Interpretation of Scripture is analogous to mystagogical initiation and catechesis. A metaphysical realism fits analogously within a cosmology opened by apocalypse. We will first look at theology as a kind of realism. Then we will look at liturgy as apocalyptic in nature, allowing us to define liturgical theology as an apocalyptic realism. After returning to the problems with liturgical theology described in the Introduction, we will conclude these discussions.

THEOLOGY AS REALISM

Theology as divine pattern recognition demands a non-reductive account of transcendence. Non-reductive accounts of transcendence are called *realism*. I must assume, for the purposes of brevity, a basic scholarly knowledge of these foundational philosophical terms. By *nominalism*, I mean the assumption that generic predicates are merely noetic abstractions, and the concomitant notion of freedom as arbitrary decision-making. For example, if I say "Joseph loves Mary," the predicate is not generic but definite. But if I say, "Joseph is good," "good," here is a generic predicate. Nominalism would claim that "good," as a generic predicate covering many possible concrete things, represents an abstraction on the part of a rational mind. Likewise, Joseph, as a concrete and discrete entity among others is only free when he can arbitrarily choose among different possible actions with regards to those discrete entities. By *realism*, I mean the assumption that generic predicates may sometimes represent abstraction, but may also indicate participation in a transcendent reality or archetype, and the concomitant notion that freedom and the realization of ends define one another. For example, if I say, "chairs are furniture," most later realists would affirm that "furniture" indeed refers to an abstraction of rational human minds from a set of possible human artifacts. However, if I say "Joseph is good," the word "good," here is not merely an abstraction, rather, it refers to a transcendent reality or archetype in which many things, Joseph included, can participate and, through behavior, manifest. Likewise, Joseph, as an entity that may participate in and manifest transcendent realities, finds freedom in pursuing participation in the highest possible realities for which he has been made suitable.

Mention of realism brings up for many, as modern Western Christians, the fear of that great bogey, Platonism, as the problem of early Christian syncretism. I lean on the great patristic scholar Robert Louis Wilken for aid here:

> The notion that the development of early Christian thought represented a Hellenization of Christianity has outlived its usefulness. The time has come to bid a fond farewell to the ideas of Adolf von Harnack, the nineteenth-century historian of dogma whose thinking has influenced the interpretation of early Christian thought for more than a century.[1]

---

1. Wilken, *Spirit of Early Christian Thought*, xvi.

Wilken places yet another nail in the coffin of the surprisingly still popular nineteenth-century notion that Christianity formed some kind of dialectic opposition to Hellenism. I nevertheless deliberately use the word *realism* as opposed to Platonism in an attempt to avert some of these worries. Let us reject, together with the church fathers, any flatfooted adoption of Plato's thought or that of his followers.

Nevertheless, what modern scholars call "middle Platonism" was simply the philosophical *koine* at the time of the birth of the gospel into the world—and what we call "philosophy" in the West was nothing more nor less than the "theology" of the pagans.[2] Philosophy is a way of life before it is a mode of discourse.[3] It is a mode of discourse as the analogical counterpart to a total way of life. Behavior precedes discourse. And in this sense theology and philosophy are one. Philosophy is simply pagan, pre-Christian theology. Christian theology is the practice of disciplined love of Wisdom.

Whatever we may assume a given Platonism to be or to mean, the fundamental insight of all Platonisms is just this: patterns can be real and not always mere projections of a (human) mind. There is plenty of projection going on, hence the need for philosophy and theology to dispel our illusions. If some patterns are real then they are explanatorily prior to any particular manifestation. Granting this explanatory priority is the only way that the recognition of a pattern can grant any knowledge, any grasp of reality, once discerned. For if patterns are merely projection, or mere epiphenomenon of matter, or some combination of the two, then pattern recognition grants no real knowledge. Projection alone does not put us in touch with reality. Epiphenomena are reducible or at least arbitrary. But patterns are sometimes real and sometimes recognizable. If this is the case, then the noetic is enfolded within the ontic, and knowledge follows reality. Plato ruminated upon the above commitments through what has come to be called his "theory of forms." But one need not hold anything like a theory of forms to be a realist, a Platonist. All one must do is concede to the above logic.[4]

Patterns are real, not just ideas in the mind. Patterns transcend their various manifestations and may manifest on multiple levels simultaneously. Pattern recognition is about noticing analogous relationships between a dynamic reality and its manifestation in various media. Another

2. See Jenson, "Gratia non tollit."

3. See Hadot, *What is Ancient Philosophy?* and *Philosophy as a Way of Life.*

4. See Gerson, *From Plato to Platonism.*

word for analogy is proportion. Proportion, mathematically speaking, is the relationship of two variables whose ratio is constant. Ratios are quantitative analogies. Analogues are qualitative or geometric ratios. The word *proportion*, when used as a noun, is a part, a share, or a number considered in comparative relation to a whole. When *proportion* is used as a verb, it means "to adjust" or "to regulate" something so as to achieve a particular suitable relationship to something else.

We have the power to project proportionality—real and imagined. Both moral and theoretical reasoning follow this same pattern—for both good and ill. Reason, *ratio*, is about making things fit, it is about proportioning, as a verb. This fitting of things usually means making new things fit into previously acknowledged or assumed fittings, reasonings. Reason recognizes appropriate proportions and matches up to them. Reason therefore has the capacity to acknowledge and make sense of change while noticing unchangeable realities.

When the primary epistemological distinction is that of ideas to facts, as under modern nominalism, then facts and values are disconnected. The idea side of that dichotomy becomes the only side on which to place value, thus forcing an unnecessarily subjective vision of the nature of value.[5] We may contrast this epistemology with that of a pre- or even non-modern realism where patterns are the behaviors of concrete realities on a higher plane or at a deeper level of nesting. Manifestations are concrete encounters with the patterns. Under such terms there are, in the end, simply no brute facts. Values, too, line up with patterns—higher-level concrete realities manifesting at the level one currently finds oneself aware. Realism may acknowledge with nominalism the truth that anything real is necessarily concrete. But patterns do not represent abstractions. Patterns are the manifestation in media at lower levels of reality or cosmos of concrete realities and their dynamics and relationships at higher levels of reality or cosmos. In other words, realism acknowledges transcendence, rather than reifying abstraction.

A focus on the epistemological distinction of facts and ideas leads to a search for immanent causal chains. In liturgical scholarship, this often means searching for historical or cultural causation. Because when the pattern-manifestation dialectic is flattened out and forced to fit into an immanent mold, pattern is usually forced into idea, and manifestation into fact. Thus, the endearingly modern mistaken criticism of the impossibility

5. See Taylor, *A Secular Age*. See also Diagram D, in the appendix.

of Plato's heaven of forms. If the forms are merely ideations, then, of course, Plato's theory of forms is ridiculous. Fortunately, this notion that Plato's forms are abstractions is far from the truth.

An emphasis on theological pattern recognition will appear merely ideational to an imagination restricted by the fact-idea distinction, unable or unwilling to acknowledge the pattern-manifestation dialectic.[6] A take on the overall approach of this book, if interpreted under such a nominalist epistemology, will likely result in one of two criticisms, or both: that the theology does not sufficiently acknowledge the particular, or that it fails sufficiently to trace out the history of the idea or to discern its limiting cultural matrix. But if we acknowledge the reality of the pattern-manifestation dialectic, then the story changes. In fact, we come to realize that we cannot recognize concrete manifestations—not even whether our *ideations concerning* those manifestations are accurate or adequate—if we fail to discern the pattern and its transcendence over any given, particular manifestation. Secular history and anthropology cannot, methodologically speaking, acknowledge transcendence. And even if the discipline is post-critical, the best it can do is recognize that those indigenous to, or their accounts emic within, the point-of-view under study *believe*, or show that they believe, that they are coming in contact with transcendence—and, who knows? It might be true. But theology can acknowledge transcendence. And that is its chief task.

LITURGY AS APOCALYPSE

Apocalypse reveals. Liturgy, as ritual analogy, is a behavioral apocalypse. In the Christian tradition, apocalypse reveals the pattern of a temple-mythos manifest through the medium of the cosmos, and in and as both a literary genre and, importantly for this discussion, a ritual tradition. The liturgy is an apocalypse that opens up for us divine patterns for recognition. These patterns are not only separable from the media in which we find them but they exceed them and logically precede them. Otherwise, the liturgy is either projection or an epiphenomenon.[7] The Christian apocalypse reveals

---

6. See Upton, *Folk Metaphysics*. We are not trapped in history and the need for historical continuity of an idea. Nor do we need the reconstruction of a supposed "origin" of an idea. We are going for the recognizable archetype across ephemeral historical manifestations.

7. Affirming the reality of Christian ritual affirms Christian (apocalyptic) realism.

an economy. Apocalypse reveals a "plan" for the distribution of God's gifts to all God's children. The divine economy is, in fact, both *that which is revealed* and *that which reveals*.

The term *apocalypse* comes from the book attributed to John the Elder that ends the new covenant Scriptures. All other such literature in the Holy Scriptures and now, even extra-canonical literature that is similar in style, has, by extension, received that same name of *apocalypse*. Apocalypse has developed the connotation of a radically imminent eschatology. But a strong scholarly line has held an alternative position for some time now.[8] The key to apocalypse is the unveiling of the unity of heaven and earth in God's plan—and that especially in the face of distress due to (the perception of) the rupture between heaven and earth, a tear in God's plan.

The rupture, or perceived rupture, between heaven and earth is both epistemic and ontic in nature. It is epistemic in nature insofar as we have lost the ability, through the fall, to see that heaven and earth are simply, in fact, one. For in God and according to the divine will, they are, and ever will, remain one. It is ontological in nature insofar as the fall has actually caused a rupture within the cosmos itself. Finally, the rupture of heaven and earth is, in an important sense, epistemic and ontic, indeed ontic because epistemic. Because of the role of being human as priest of the cosmos, our *epistemic* loss itself causes or contributes to the ongoing ontic rupture between heaven and earth. So, which is it? Ontic, epistemic, ontic because epistemic? For they seem to contradict one another or, at the very least, not to be able to be held simultaneously. A Christian realism, however, recognizes ontology and epistemology as nested realities. Holding to this seeming contradiction is part of the paradox of the Christian mystery and the revelation of the apocalyptic nature of Scripture.

Apocalypse in canonical literature, as well as much of the various mythological writings that survive from the ANE, is the discourse that corresponds to the liturgy of the temple. In liturgy, something is revealed. In this case, the liturgy reveals the same thing that is revealed, discursively, through apocalyptic literature. That is to say, liturgy is a ritual action that

---

This must be so, otherwise the low-church Protestants, such as, for example, our Quaker brothers and sisters, are all too correct, and sacraments ought to be abandoned as quickly as possible as superfluous, and perhaps even misleading and damningly pernicious.

8. See Rowland, *Open Heaven*. This is an early and already summative work in the shift from understanding apocalyptic literature to be primarily catastrophically eschatological to being more immanent political criticism in light of the unity of visible and invisible realities.

unveils, through its enactment, the unity of heaven and earth in God's plan. Many anthropologists would point out the correspondence between rite and myth in human behavior in general. The liturgy and apocalypse are their Christian instance.

Because liturgy is ritual apocalypse, liturgy is something simultaneously received from above and from ancestors. That something apocalyptic would be received from above may seem obvious, but in the face of critical reduction this demands a faith in revelation and inspiration that entails a non-competitive authorship on the part of God. That something apocalyptic is received from ancestors may seem contrary to its nature. But, in fact, the cosmos revealed in apocalyptic literature is always the cosmos as inherited in previous vision. These cumulative scriptural visions match up well to still more ancient Near Eastern cosmologies in general.[9] Strange new goings-on in heaven or on earth may be recorded, but what remains consistent throughout the literature is the reality and unity of heaven and earth, their perceived disunity on the part of human beings on earth, that God sits in counsel, holds court, receives worship and service, celebrates a festival sacrifice in celebration of the resolution of the cosmic crisis, and that God has a plan to bring heavenly order to earth.

The ritual activity that unveils the unity of heaven and earth in God's plan unveils that plan to be a sacrifice for the benefit of the economy of a city-state—the kingdom of God. Thus, we find the deep connection between the apocalyptic and the cosmological topography of our liturgy. Each of the chapters of this book described liturgy as apocalyptic from some given angle, from some level of scale, or along a certain medium.[10]

What, then, is the mystical reality of the Christian mystery? Mystery is the revelation of God's plan for the final state of God's cosmos, when she has reached and fulfilled her telos: the union of heaven and earth with one another and that cosmos as a whole with her Creator. The mystery, as found in the use of St. Paul,[11] is the revelation, the apocalypse, of God's plan for this union and reunion. The Christian mystery both constitutes and reveals—constitutes through its revelation of—the fundamental archetypal and eschatological harmony of God and cosmos, heaven and earth. And ancient Hebrew apocalypse is a literature that corresponds to mystagogy:

---

9. See Pritchard, *The Ancient Near East.*

10. Recall the example of the stereogram from the Introduction.

11. I am thinking especially of Romans, the Corinthian correspondences, Ephesians, Colossians, and the Pastorals.

heaven and earth are revealed as one in God's plan. It is the inspired liturgical theology of Scripture.

The Christian liturgy is Christian ritual analogy. And that analogical
behavior, just like all apocalyptic behavior, simultaneously veils and unveils
its mystery. Central to Christian revelation is the role of apocalypse in re-
vealing the unity (or, perhaps, reuniting) of heaven and earth in the face of
their perceived (again, perhaps actual) dissonance. Thus, any full discussion of liturgy requires us to relate liturgy to apocalypse (organic analogue)
and cosmology (created reality).

Liturgy performs a mystical initiation—that embodied pattern that
inaugurates contemplation. Liturgy is the somatic medium of our human
contemplation of the divine. It provides our constant, reliable, assured contact with the subject matter of our discourse: God. For contemplation is
that behavior that renders us most like God, and, therefore, able to resonate
with God, tune in, listen, and discern transcendent patterns in immanent
manifestation.

The temple-mythos that forms the background of apocalyptic ritual
and literature entails the ancient modus operandi, shared by many differing philosophies and local cults, that earthly realities participate in and
(sometimes willy-nilly, e.g., apocalyptic literature, especially) manifest
heavenly realities that transcend them. Plato's philosophy expresses such
a mode of being in the world, but is not its only or even ultimate (ancient)
expression.[12] For example, figurative reading of Scripture assumes a realism because apocalyptic is itself an example of ancient realism—it assumes
access to, and possibility of knowledge of, transcendent patterns that are
real and that transcend our mundane order. Plato's dialogues and ancient
apocalypses shared a similar background with regard to relating heavenly
to earthly realities. They are parallel literary structures within the ancient
Mediterranean basin that cut across cultural-linguistic differences. It is not
about the philosophical system or mode of expression per se, but a cosmos
in which there are chains of reality that permeate, participate in, and manifest one another.

Plato gave the Greeks a way to relate the transcendent to the immanent, the heavens and the earth, eventually the eternal to the temporal,
without reduction to, nor simple rejection of, received mythology.[13] And
that is exactly what apocalyptic literature also does for Israel: it reveals in a

12. See Mazza, *Mystagogy*, 168.
13. See Brisson, *Plato the Myth Maker*.

mystery the real heavens, subordinating all other gods to Israel's God, and breaks down the ANE myths from within. What Plato does for the Greeks, God grants Israel through apocalypse. Christianity inherits this apocalyptic tradition and proclaims its fulfillment in Christ and its local manifestation in the martyrs and the ritual mysteries. Behold, the new creation. A Christian realism provides a means to talk about transcendence and the heavenly (i.e., the supernal) without being polytheistic or naively mythological on the one hand, or reductionist or dismissive on the other.[14]

It is no coincidence that the philosopher who combined Parmenides and Heraclites through Pythagoras should also have been initiated into the Elysian Mysteries. As ancient philosophy was pre-Christian theology,[15] Plato, together with Pythagoras and others like him, was one of the first liturgical theologians. Our dispute with him as Christians may have more to do with the liturgy he was reflecting upon than with the technicalities of his metaphysic. But from a fundamental anthropological point of view Plato was a liturgical theologian nonetheless.

If Christian realism inherits anything uncritically from Plato it is this: the transcendent cannot be comprehended in human words or even with human minds.[16] We do not meet the transcendent in the form of straight-forward noetic *content*, but as noetic *formation*. It is not what we see, but a different way of seeing: illumination. Our eyes remain human, our vision is transformed.[17] The return to mystery in our liturgies after liturgical renewal demands a realistic interpretation lest, if construed as mere human construct, it should fall into manipulation for immanent ends. The liturgy, if it is liturgy at all, may never serve as a community-building exercise—however much it may or may not build human community—nor may it serve as a clever subversive model for an education committee—however much it may well teach, through its very enactment, the faith that saves.

---

14. For Schmemann, the loss of the centrality of eschatological discourse (the Christian "myth") in the West forms the direct antecedent to scholasticism. This is a realist claim. The ritual action of the liturgy is a ritual apocalypse, a ritual unveiling of *eschatic* realities *in and through* the very actions themselves. For this particular insight into Schmemann's approach I am indebted to Fagerberg's lecture, "The Cost of Understanding Schmemann in the West."

15. See Jenson, "Gratia non tollit."

16. We thus avoid either a naïve realism on the one hand or a so-called "metaphysics of presence" on the other. See Ricoeur, *Interpretation Theory* and Derrida *Writing and Difference*.

17. See Austin Farrer, *The Glass of Vision*.

LITURGICAL THEOLOGY AS APOCALYPTIC REALISM

For liturgical theology to have any real traction as a discipline, and in order to keep it from falling into ritual theory on the one hand, or mere theological gloss on liturgical historiography on the other, liturgical theology needs to fit into the frame of a transcendent metaphysic that engages ritual as something that unveils higher realities.[18] Forms, patterns, are real because of the way in which the cosmos works—and not only the cosmos, but also because of the way in which *anthropos* works as the nested microcosm within the cosmos. These patterns transfer through media. Liturgy is a medium that discloses divine patterns. I call this *apocalyptic realism*.

We encounter reality, God, and the world he has made, as, although transcendent, nevertheless real and knowable. We respond with analogous behavior: we worship God, liturgically, together with the surrounding transcendent, but still created, cosmos—the angels. The behavior itself opens out for us, apocalyptically, in a mystery, the very realities to which they respond. Our discourse thus follows our behavior. Liturgical theology becomes an apocalyptic realism. Liturgical theology is the retrieval of an epistemology of transcendent pattern recognition as opposed to representational ideation theorizing external facts.

Understanding God in terms of some abstract category of being places God as a constituent member of a genre that proves higher in explanatory power. Such an explanatory move will never do in any truly monotheistic tradition. Theology since at least Karl Barth, and especially in some of his North American post-critical followers, answers this problem of ontology through a now famous rejection of ontology. John Zizioulas, in his work *Being as Communion*,[19] offers a different solution to the relationship of ontology (being) to theology (God) that keeps ontology, but subordinates it to theology.

Instead of understanding God in terms of being, Zizioulas attempts to understand being in terms of God—a God who precedes it logically, but whose life is coterminous with being itself. Instead of essence, existence, substance, or accident as the fundamental terminology of his ontology, Zizioulas makes *person* and *communion* his key ontological terms—terms that find their primary meaning in theology. Person is the fundamental

18. Hans Boersma's work to date effectively argues this line. He summarizes his argument both for Christian realism and that the retrieval of Christian realism was a key constituent of the *Nouvelle Théologie* in his *Heavenly Participation*.

19. Zizioulas, *Being as Communion*, 65.

unit of reality for Zizioulas. Persons do not exist without other persons. Thus, the Father and the eternal processions of the Son and the Spirit are simultaneous realities to one another. The communion, the fellowship, that these fundamental, infinite persons share is what we truly mean when we utter the word "being." Being *is* communion. Zizioulas has attempted a theological reduction, or, at least, profound redefinition of ontology. The ontology is relational, personal, not abstract or substantial. Without going into further detail here, I want fundamentally to concur with Zizioulas' bold move.[20] This work in no small part represents an attempt to build a Christian cosmology from an ontology indebted to Zizioulas.

Although Zizioulas does the tradition a great service in his radical reversal of the usual order of theology to ontology, and he relates all this most magnificently to eschatology and ecclesiology, the missing piece is a fully developed, a fully retrieved, Christian cosmology. What is that dynamic that generates the patterns that echo up and down the varying media of created reality? Persons in communion generate patterns that transfer across media and resonate up and down levels of scale. Created pure intelligences—the angels—generate their cosmic patterns. Human beings, "a little lower than the angels," generate their patterns in habits, customs, and cultures. Ultimately, Father, Son, and Holy Spirit live in a dynamic pattern of mutual communion spilling out eternal, infinite chains of spiraling patterns unto ages of ages.

Now, to clarify, *person* is not, necessarily, something with human-like psychological states or some center of subjectivity or consciousness. Going with Boethius's classic definition,[21] but parsing in more contemporary terms, what I mean here by *person* is an isolable instance of rational telos, where *rational* indicates the expression of proportionality or balance in the face of relationship that allows for communion. To say, therefore, that angels or even the Godhead itself are *persons* is not to say that they enjoy some kind of human psychological experience or that they are simply, straight-

---

20. Although the vision I present here is deeply indebted to Zizioulas's important contribution, I want to distance myself from one dominant theme in *Being as Communion*—his persistent voluntarist notion of freedom. His points about ontology and their relationship to theology, however, still hold even if his voluntarism is rejected. In fact, one could argue, his points become all the more sound within a teleological account of freedom and volition. But that is another study.

21. A person is an individual subsistence (or, substance) of rational nature. See Boethius, *A Treatise*. Although Aquinas would nuance this, Boethius's definition remains foundational to Western theology.

forwardly, single instances of conscious subjectivity. In other words, we are using the word *person* here in a theological way and avoiding anthropomorphism. Who knows what it is to be a god? The dynamic enactment of the relationships among persons thus defined generates patterns where the word *pattern* indicates intelligible, discernible, e.g., isolable interpersonal dynamics (and that often expressible in terms of a ratio). Knowledge under such conditions represents the manifestations of a noetic analogue to this ontic proportion; thus knowledge is pattern recognition.

Assuming an ontology of persons in communion allows their dynamic patterns to be the forms Plato and his disciples discerned. Plato's ontology, without the revelation of a non-competitive transcendent Creator, may represent a projection onto ontology from a nevertheless accurately discerned cosmology. I would like to suggest that Plato's so-called theory of forms is primarily a cosmological, not ontological, insight. Plato took the cosmological insight that higher patterns (behaviors) manifest at lower cosmic levels (as events) as grounds for the relationship of subject to predicate and then leaped to the ontological reality of forms over instances. This seems to me a not unreasonable mistake without an ontology of persons in communion already in place.

With the revelation of a non-competitive transcendent God who is not coterminous with creation, but nevertheless who shares his being with it, we are able to "baptize" the Western tradition of metaphysical realism and keep its insights about forms or patterns cosmological, rather than ontological or theological in nature. For if what are most real are persons in communion, and theology thus grounds ontology, then an ontology of communion grounds a dynamic cosmology. In this realist cosmology, the dynamic relationship of persons in communion becomes the patterns we discern and the "fields"[22] in which cosmological realities manifest.

So Plato's realism, within a Christian context, with the gift of a greater apocalyptic revelation of the nature of things, turns out to be more cosmic than ontic in primary insight with regards to the relationship of pattern to manifestation. We have thus performed a reversal, an anagogical reversal of analogy. Where ontology fits into theology, and the cosmos fits into being

---

22. See Alexander, *Notes on the Synthesis of Form*. Alexander's theory of design holds that concrete objects, such as tools, articles of furniture, houses, even cities manifest as the necessary material realities to solve problems generated by the dynamic fields of concrete human behavior patterns. Alexander's theory of design provides us with just the insight we need to connect cosmology with Zizioulas's ontology.

itself, analogically and dynamically. In fact, the very nested nature of reality grounds and demands our rational task of anagogy.

We also find a reprieve from fears about Plato's ontological hierarchy. If Plato's insights are primarily cosmological, rather than ontological, then what we have is a cosmological, not ontological, hierarchy. And a cosmological hierarchy is not only compatible with Christian theology, but part of the Christian revelation. The only ontological hierarchy that remains is that of created as opposed to uncreated persons, finite as opposed to infinite persons. However, in terms of their manifestation in heaven and earth, there is an echoing chain and overlapping, nested continua of cosmological hierarchies.

So, on the one hand, Plato's forms, or what I have called *patterns*,[23] are concrete, but at a higher cosmological level than our sensible existence. When in a state of grace, sustained by the flowing gift-exchange of the divine economy, higher levels within the cosmos exist in a non-competitive relationship with those realities inferior to them. They may manifest themselves and influence lower forms without disturbing the integrity of the lower. Only under conditions of the fall does competition and hegemony enter in. On the other hand, the patterns are immutable with respect to the realm of the sensible, but, like the astronomical heavens from whence Plato first built his anagogy to the realm of forms, they are immutably dynamic. That is to say, the dynamic of their relationship is from everlasting to everlasting, growing from glory to glory, but ever recognizable as what they are, and from whom they proceed.

Even though Plato's forms are dynamic, they remain impersonal and continue the pre-Socratic project of demythologization. Plato nevertheless avoids the material reductionism of the pre-Socratic philosophers of his inheritance. With an apocalyptic realism, patterns become the dynamics of relationship and the behaviors inherent to their enactment at whatever plane of reality they may manifest. It understands that the dynamic patterns

---

23. I prefer to use *pattern* to *form* or *idea*. Idea connotes the subjective. Form connotes the static cookie-cutter. Pattern evokes something more dynamic, like a Mandelbrot set. And, like a Mandelbrot set, there is the mathematical reality regardless of abstract systems of mathematical notation, the current accepted abstract notation and then the various and pluriform physical representations and even manifestations. They pass away, but the Mandelbrot set remains. Nevertheless, it would be odd to describe it as a "static" rather than "dynamic" reality, as it just exactly describes a pattern of recursive and performative unfolding. See http://mathworld.wolfram.com/MandelbrotSet.html for more on the Mandelbrot set.

are about relationship among persons, and that the unfolding of those patterns in the sensible realm takes place over time.

The Christian realism I suggest here is therefore not static and formal, but dynamic and personal, where the dynamic patterns generated by the liturgy of the angels, created but incorporeal persons, replace the impersonal forms of Plato. This apocalyptic realism is not abstract, but concrete. What gives it explanatory power is the positing of different but interacting planes of reality. And the heavens are populated, peopled, or, rather *personed* and thus not vacant or simply crammed with the static furniture of abstraction. The heavens are populated with angels.[24] The angels and the dynamic liturgy they enact replace the abstract and static forms of (misunderstood) Platonism.[25]

This apocalyptic critique of mythology is both more permissive and more strict than that of Plato's. Plato banishes the gods from heaven. Apocalypse allows the gods to remain in heaven. But the myths are not just morally criticized, as they are with Plato. Apocalypse reveals the gods themselves to be relegated to mere angelic status, messengers of the One. Apocalypse resituates the corrupting myths of paganism within a temple-mythos of holy and reasonable worship before the One who is beyond the cosmos and is its ground, source, and telos. The field of communion among created persons and between them and their uncreated God produces a plenitude of, nevertheless, isolable patterns. These patterns manifest between persons and leave behind "residue" at each cosmological level of remove. Hence, the physical world is the material artifact of the heavenly liturgy. Thus, apocalyptic Scripture in its Semitic literary genre criticizes myth by myth in a way analogous to, parallel with, and yet superior to Plato's own Hellenistic myth-making critique of myth.[26]

A personal ontology focuses on communion and interconnection. Now *anthropos* nests within cosmos. And our chief mode of human participation is that of contemplation. In our psychosomatic nature, contemplation involves the body along its continuum as an apropos medium of divine revelation (reductive accounts not withstanding). Bodies cannot exist without flow of nourishment, provision. The cycle and flow of a gift economy is the corporate analogue to the circulatory system in a given corporal body.

---

24. See Louth, "Platonism in the Middle English Mystics."
25. Plato's forms are neither abstract nor static.
26. See Brisson, *Plato the Myth-maker.*

The economy of the gift is about communion—the distribution of needs to those who share a body. These patterns of distribution render descending and ascending chains of manifestations across media and their relative continua. "We are climbing Jacob's ladder." Economy is all about proportioning. Economics and metaphysics are inherently implicated in one another. Communion is the redistribution of increase across the body-corporate. The collection for Jerusalem was, for Paul, therefore, the eschatological fulfillment of the desire of the nations.[27] The prophecy of Israel becoming a light to the nations (Isa 60:3) would be fulfilled therein: all nations sacrificing to the God of heaven, in Jerusalem. The distributive economy of the temple in Jerusalem would now, through the new covenant, finally come to pass as the nations lent their aid to the struggling body of faithful in the holy city. The divine economy manifests on earth.

When we retrieve the hive, that is to say, genuine corporate embodiment—the kind of genuine corporate embodiment dependent upon and enabled by the liturgical economy of the gift—we lose nominalism. Christian theologians, one would hope, would be prone to validate the reality of corporate bodies. But it is not in vogue to talk that way within the confines of nominalist academia. Why? Because of what nominalism does to bodies. Nominalism is the discourse that corresponds to the behavior of late-modern individualism, voluntarism, and consumerism. It grants us individuals, impermeable selves, homunculi "using" bodies in "excarnation."[28]

If philosophy is a way of life, then nominalism must be a way of life. And it is. Nominalism is voluntarism, individualism, the artificial creation of the so-called public sphere, rejection of tradition, social and political constructivism, and, increasingly, consumerism.[29] It is a liturgy we are all, in the West, swept up into, willy-nilly, from shopping malls to junk mail. Apocalyptic realism is also a way of life. Its chief disciplines are liturgy and asceticism. Liturgy is an essential part of the way of life called Christianity. It forms an alternative way of life in the face of modern human degradation.[30]

---

27. Acts 20; 2 Cor 8, etc.

28. See Taylor, *A Secular Age.*

29. Hoff, "The Rise and Fall." For the tyranny of secondary, and even tertiary discourse in the academy, see Steiner, *Real Presences.*

30. To use a more mundane analogy, healthy folks eat organic food; perhaps healthy folks would prefer a more organic economy as well—the divine economy of a liturgical community.

DENYS AS EXEMPLAR

Liturgical theology encourages somatic enactment leading to contemplation,[31] rather than representation leading to ideology.[32] Denys the Pseudo-Areopagite[33] provides an example for liturgical theology that is neither systematic nor totalizing. He is a shared figure in both the Eastern and Western Christian traditions. His work is contemplative in tone, exegetical in nature, and assumes and meditates upon and within a ritual context.[34] Envisioning Denys as a model means envisioning the possibility of theology engaged as primary, rather than what post-critics would call secondary theology or even the tertiary discourse of modern scholarship.

So, for example, Denys's contemplative vision of Isaiah 6 ends in a conundrum. For his theology of angels cannot allow for the seraphim to do anything other than contemplate the divine. And yet the Scriptures clearly describe the seraphim as performing a task commanded by the Lord. So after contemplating the entire hierarchy of the heavenly hosts, after discussing many different ways to reconcile the paradox of the theophany, Denys ends on a note of humility, with a tone made possible when the goal is contemplation, rather than ideation:

> [I]t is up to your intelligence and your critical understanding to decide on one or another of the solutions to the problem referred to, accepting it as more likely, more reasonable, and hence closer to the truth. Unless, of course, you yourself have a solution closer to the real truth or have learned it from someone else. . . . And then you might be able to reveal to me . . . a contemplation which is clearer and thus more beloved to me.[35]

Not only does he submit that his contemplation is not definitive, he asks for a better one from his reader. Denys assumes that the cosmos and her God infinitely exceed the human capacity for their contemplation— and certainly, therefore, any one particular example of contemplation. A Christian realism is not a totalizing endeavor—that is the nominalist task of exhaustive system. A Christian realism invites a never-ending dialogue

31. By "somatic enactment," see Emminghaus' *Wesen* in *The Eucharist*.

32. See Hoff, *The Analogical Turn*.

33. I could just as well have chosen Maximus the Confessor as an exemplar, as well as several others.

34. See Louth, *Denys the Areopagite*.

35. Pseudo-Dionysius, *The Complete Works*, 308.

with Scripture in the ritual mysteries knowing that transcendent realms will echo up and down cosmic spheres and across the pluriform media of God's created plenitude. We have only to be willing to submit theory to *theoria*.

THEOLOGIA PRIMA AND THE PROBLEM OF LITURGICAL THEOLOGY

Recall from the introduction how Kavanagh contributes to liturgical theology the phrase *theologia prima* and the approach to theology it warrants. Some scholarship has brought up doubts about Kavanagh's famous phrase.[36] In translating Schmemann into the West, Kavanagh asserts that the liturgy itself is a key, perhaps *the* key theological act. *Actions speak louder than words*. Yes. And the metaphor of Christian action as theological statement is an important, even liturgical theological insight. But theology in popular parlance indicates something primarily discursive in nature. I believe this semantic equivocation has, in part, blocked Kavanagh's reception of Schmemann from wider distribution among other Western theologians. We may be able to move through this impasse if, instead, we note that the church's liturgy is not primarily discursive, but enacted, behavioral, ritual in nature.

If liturgy is *theologia prima*, then to what does a theologian truly refer when uttering the word *liturgy*? What is a properly *theological*, and not simply historical or anthropological, referent for that word? I have presented a vision of liturgy as a human behavior analogous to the divine economy. What is the central meaning or task indicated by the word *theology*? I have presented theology as the anagogical unity of the divine nature, contemplation, and the interpretation of Holy Scripture. How might these mutually define one another? Theology is the discerning of transcendent patterns; liturgy is the media in which we discern those patterns. Liturgical theology is economic anagogy. Liturgical theology is an apocalyptic realism.

"When believers come to worship on a Sunday morning, they do not come with their minds a *tabula rasa*."[37] Such a point shows a semantic gap between historical and theological study of liturgy, or, perhaps simply a

---

36. Most of these come from historians and I cannot engage their chief arguments in this brief chapter. See Aune, "Liturgy and Theology."

37. Aune "Liturgy and Theology", 53, quoting Paul Bradshaw, "Difficulties in Doing," 191.

category error. *Theologia prima* is not about whether any one individual or even group of individuals in a local church is *aware* that liturgy precedes theology. It is about squares and rectangles. Not all behavior is discourse, but all discourse is behavior. Behavior is primary, discourse is a kind of behavior, and, although necessary, still a lesser part of behavior as a whole. It is a logical, not a chronological claim.

Not only liturgical theology, but also the Liturgical Renewal Movement that preceded and enabled it, assumed a sound anthropological point: behavior logically and categorically precedes discourse, discourse itself being an example of behavior. This is the real depth of *theologia prima*, and the reason why, in the face of much historical criticism, liturgical theologians still seem to cling to something historically moot. But the point was always anthropological, rather than historical in nature.

The key to retaining the importance of what is behind the commitment to liturgy as *theologia prima* is the shift from a static, atomizing metaphysics toward a dynamic, relational metaphysic; from a flat, nominalist metaphysic to realism. I have shown in the above chapters how liturgy is *theologia prima* manifesting across various media and levels of scale. The liturgy is the divine economy. Liturgy is *theologia prima* because *leitourgia* is *oikonomia prima*. And the divine economy manifests and reveals the divine nature, theology proper. All other aspects nest within this economic foundation. Liturgy is a manifestation on earth of the divine economy of the heavens. Liturgy is initiation into the divine mystery. Liturgy is corporate contemplation through ritual apocalypse. It is the interpretation of Scripture through its ritual enactment. And through all of the above the liturgy places us in contact with God, within the dynamic life of a God who *is* contemplation.

One problem in translating these insights into a modern theological context is that ritual initiation is simply not identical with mystagogy as a whole. Anthropologically speaking, we must enter into the mysteries, somatically, but then we must also receive the *catechetical* mystagogy that forms its noetic counterpart for the mind. We must be led—body, will (ascesis), and mind—into the Christian mystery. Liturgy, in this sense, is *doctrina prima* more than *theologia prima*. Liturgical theology is catechetical, or discursive mytagogy: discourse concerning the mystical realities unveiled through participation in the ritual mysteries. Our Western emphasis on the centrality of ideational system or noetic dogmatics as the key connotation (if not definition) of *theology* keeps our academic theological tradition from receiving the gift of liturgical theology.

The point, of course, is not to present liturgical theology as a new, better, shinier, set of sources, or methods, of academic theology. The point is that we have already derailed Christian theology when we begin to talk in such terms. Source is the nominalist attempt to replace the role that apocalypse, imagination, and participation formerly played in Christian thought. Method, likewise, is the nominalist attempt to replace discipline, ascesis, contemplation, *theosis*. Such replacements are fitting to an excarnate, voluntarist world of individuals. But they do not fit Christianity.

Other liturgical theological conundrums find resolution when placed within the ancient understanding of the nature of theology as the unity of the divine nature, contemplation, and interpretation and the nature of the cosmos as analogous, nested continua, with the capacity to resonate with divine pattern. Realism entails levels of scale across the cosmos and differing media even within those levels. The Christian cosmos is not a flat universe. Thus, we will be able to nest our human discourse about liturgy into the deepest possible continuum of theological contemplation. This nesting of the medium of liturgy into the pattern of a trinitarian economy performs an approach to *theologia prima* that answers recent scholarly controversy. An apocalyptic realism adds the necessary dimension to cut through some of these Gordian Knots.

Recall how two sets of worries about liturgical theology, often voiced by the same parties, were interestingly contrary to one another: the fear that liturgical theology was simultaneously too abstract with regard to its liturgical studies while being too concrete and local with regard to its theological aspirations. Denying transcendent participation forces theology to choose between mere metaphor or blank literalism. Without a transcendent and analogical approach to the relationship of patterns and media we mistake and conflate the two, usually in the direction of immanent flattening. We do not need to contrast, for example, law to gospel if we have a grace that sustains our nature, a God in whom we "live and move and have our being." In a cosmic-project that imagines overlapping transcendent planes that mutually penetrate and manifest one another, we are allowed the third option that is not a compromise between the two, but a way beyond them. Anagogy through apocalyptic realism gives us the capacity to distinguish the pattern we discern from the various media in which we discern it. The pattern is the divine economy—itself fitting to the Triune life of God. One key medium in which we discern this pattern is our own, human liturgy.

How do we give due reverence to the particular and the concrete with respect to liturgy, whether diachronically through historical study, or synchronically through anthropology or sociology (ritual theory)? Such a questions corresponds to the general worry that liturgical theology floats too free of the historical and the concrete.[38] How could this approach to mystagogy and liturgical theology honor modern historical consciousness? How could it honor the fact that God heals history through a temporal incarnation?

The relationship of mystagogy, proper to mystagogical catechesis provides an exact analogue to the worries with regard to the project of liturgical theology as a whole. The questions asked assume that the particular and the concrete are in conflict with that which theology studies—that they are in competition with one another. Studies of immanent realities and their origins in terms of concrete chains of immanent, earthly causality in no way conflict with theology's task of discerning the manifestation of transcendent, heavenly patterns therein. It is a category error to think so. The pattern discerned in Christian theology is not abstract, it is real and concrete—the most concrete reality possible: Father, Son, and Holy Spirit. Because it is transcendent, it is not discursively exhaustible. Contemplation is potentially infinite. Hence, again, the lasting place of realism in Christian theology.

But, moreover, in a theological context, without such "myth," history itself has no (transcendent) reality. It becomes "one damn thing after another." History, and concrete rites, for that matter, become real "by dint"[39] of their relationship to something that is not historical or particular. If the cosmos is a liturgy, then, like liturgy, there is both a logic and a chronologic to that rite. There is myth, and there are histories. The relationship of the performance of a rite to its ritual logic forms an analogue to the relationship of myth to history. This does not mean that theological reasoning can contradict or ignore historical and other concrete studies. It does mean that its goals and methods differ. From the point of view of Christian faith, the concrete ritual mysteries have no *historical* or concrete reality. They only

38. Such criticism is reflected in Bradshaw's accusation that liturgical theology is based upon "bad history, or no history at all," as quoted in Aune, "Liturgy and Theology, Part 2," 193.

39. Levenson, *Sinai and Zion*, 103–10.

have historical and concrete *enactment*. Their reality is *transcendent*. The job of the theologian is to study that reality, discern those patterns, and reveal where they are breaking through in Christian life and ritual.

Discernment of transcendence within immanence is not contrary to the study of the particular; on the contrary, it gives it life. Liturgical theology includes the study of the particular, the concrete, and the local—just exactly because it is concerned to discern the concrete events wherein the pattern manifests across varying media. It does not start and end there.[40] It moves from transcendent pattern through its various immanent manifestations and back again. The ground of such seemingly speculative work is found in the examination of the Christian revelation, the Holy Scriptures. And those same Scriptures are interpreted within each concrete, historical act of Christian ritual mystery.

The Christian tradition affirms that God and the realms of reality that transcend the earthly and visible—i.e., the heavens, the invisible, and their occupants—are more real than the flux and change of history this side of the *eschaton*. We expect the life of the age to come while we walk our pilgrim way in this age that is passing away. Jesus is the radical eruption of the life of the age to come into this age that is passing away. Through Jesus, God and the heavens give human life and history reality. God has become incarnate in Jesus the Messiah, but that does not *reduce* God to history, nor trap the Lord within it, any more that it reduces God to the flesh. Our temporality is honored because Jesus is the one new thing, the one thing that is not one damn thing after another. Jesus is the blessed one: "Behold, the new creation" (2 Cor 5:17), and thus the wound of history finds its healing balm.

CONCLUSION

Recall from Chapter One how what I have come to call the temple-mythos gives us the gift of material for anagogy concerning the living God. The totemic relationship between God, king, and the corporate body of a given people-group in general, and Israel in particular—one of the most common motifs of this temple-mythos—often offends modern sensibilities. The scriptural narrative does not present this harmonic relationship across levels of scale to be a problem. The above represents a kind of organic human, even cosmic state that modern liberal ideology limits our capacity to

---

40. See Fagerberg, "Theologia Prima." This would represent Fagerberg's theology "from or about" liturgy.

imagine. The problem is not even the abuse of this order by human beings, at least not primarily. The problem is the incompetence and maleficence of the angelic rule. For "our struggle is not against flesh and blood" (Eph 6:12), rather our Lord "saw Satan fall like lightning" (Luke 10:18). God's solution is to become everyone's God. First, through Israel. Then from Israel to all nations where Israel—God's firstborn—will be a light to the world. God's plan in Jesus then becomes the radically surprising way in which God makes good on this plan. Angels are subordinated to this plan. They are no longer anyone's gods. They become mere messengers. And their replacements, the people of God, become their judges on the last day.

This apocalyptic vision is good news to the poor and the oppressed. Adopting a modern myth of autonomy as opposed to heteronomy (really, teleology) as our embodiment of freedom, adopting representation (really, mere opinion from the point of view of realism) as our embodiment of knowledge, and matter as what counts as "most real" cannot, ultimately, help indigenous, marginalized people-groups who still, thankfully (if they have not been "educated" in Western liberalism and criticism) know better. Accounts that assume reductive explanations of myth, or conflate modern critique of myth with Christian apocalyptic condemnation of the gods, again, does not help. It hurts. Liturgy is warfare. We worship the lamb or we worship the beast.

A more profound and difficult set of questions would be: are any of our Eucharistic celebrations really *Eucharist*, absent a genuine corporate-body formed by a gift-exchange economy? When many of us in the Christian West experience the consumption of prepackaged wafers among relative strangers, are we "discerning the body" (1 Cor 11:28)? Are we celebrating Eucharist anymore? When we look at St. Paul's collection for the church of Jerusalem and compare it to our contemporary experience of communion under a church of divided confessionalism, do we miss the mark? When the Christians in the marginalized world suffer, when Armenians suffer genocide, when Coptic Egyptians are attacked, Syrians driven from their homes and crucified while Western Christians debate whether it makes sense to believe in resurrection anymore, have we, instead, *ritualized* the rite? Do we only perform a mockery, a ghostly shadow of a once powerful economy? Paul told the Corinthians, "it is not the Lord's Supper that you eat" (1 Cor 11:20)! Is he telling us this today? Can we listen? In the face of such questions, it is good both to recall that salvation is a gift *and that the gift empowers repentance.*

Approached through the gift of faith, ritual mystery has the power to resonate and manifest the mystical realities of the Christian encounter with God. Apocalyptic realism nests within a cosmos that is, itself, an apocalypse. Liturgical theology returns contemplation of the mystery, that is to say, theology, proper, to its chief point of contact on earth: the ritual mysteries. This is the gift, after years of modern secondary critical discourse, and now, even postmodern tertiary meta-discourse, of a genuine return to primary Christian discourse. Contemplation of the Christian ritual mysteries forms the contemplation of the Christian mystical reality itself. Liturgical theology is more than a different kind of method for academic theology, or a different starting point of reflection for Christian scholarship. Liturgical theology reawakens us to the way in which the mysteries of the Christian religion are an invitation to a way of life, a life of the age to come, lived out in this age that is passing away together with its concomitant mode of discourse, nested organically therein.

And so to the One who sits above the floods, enthroned upon the Cherubim, hymned by flaming tongues of Seraphim, be honor and glory: Father, Son, and Holy Spirit; both now and ever, and unto ages of ages. Amen.

Appendix

DIAGRAM A
Nested Continua

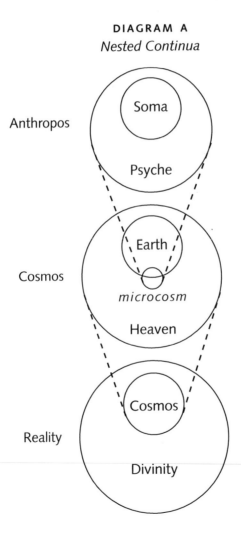

Anthropos

Soma

Psyche

Cosmos

Earth

microcosm

Heaven

Reality

Cosmos

Divinity

DIAGRAM B
Encounter, Behavior, Discourse

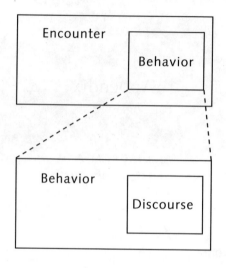

DIAGRAM C
The Somatic Continuum

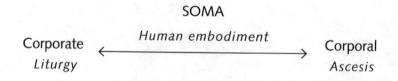

DIAGRAM D
Epistemology and Value

Realism:

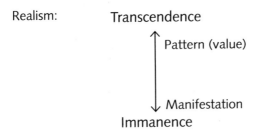

Transcendence

Pattern (value)

Manifestation
Immanence

Nominalism:

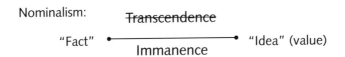

~~Transcendence~~

"Fact" ●————————————● "Idea" (value)
Immanence

Bibliography

Adam, A. K. M., et al. "Should We Be Teaching the Historical-Critical Method?" *Teaching Theology & Religion* 12, no. 2 (2009) 162–87.

Alexander, Christopher. *The Nature Of Order: An Essay on the Art of Building and the Nature of the Universe.* New York: Oxford University Press, 2001.

———. *Notes on the Synthesis of Form.* Cambridge: Harvard University Press, 1964.

———. *The Timeless Way of Building.* New York: Oxford University Press, 1979.

Alexander, Christopher, and Sara Ishikawa, Murray Silverstein, Max Jacobson, Ingrid Fiksdahl-King, Shlomo Angel. *A Pattern Language: Towns, Buildings, Construction.* New York: Oxford University Press, 1977.

Anderson, Gary. "Sacrifice and Sacrificial Offerings." In *Anchor Bible Dictionary, Vol. 5,* edited by David Noel Freedman, 870–86. New York: Doubleday, 1992.

Anselm of Canterbury. *The Major Works.* Edited by Brian Davies and G. R. Evans. Oxford: Oxford University Press, 1998.

Asals, Heather A. R. *Equivocal Predication: George Herbert's Way to God.* Toronto: University of Toronto Press, 1981.

Augustine. *Teaching Christianity.* De Doctrina Christiana. Translated by Edmund Hill, OP. Hyde Park, NY: New City, 1996.

Aune, Michael B. "The Current State of Liturgical Theology: A Plurality of Particularities." *St. Vladimir's Theological Quarterly* 53, no. 2–3 (2009) 209–29.

———. "Liturgy and Theology: Rethinking the Relationship, Part 1, Setting the Stage." *Worship* 81, no. 1 (2007) 46–68.

———. "Liturgy and Theology: Rethinking the Relationship, Part 2, A Different Starting Place." *Worship* 81, no. 2 (2007) 141–69.

Austin, Gerard. *Anointing with the Spirit: The Rite of Confirmation.* 1985. Reprint. Collegeville, MN: Liturgical, 2004.

———, et al. *Eucharist: Toward the Third Millennium.* Chicago: Liturgy Training, 2007.

———, ed. *Fountain of Life.* Washington, DC: Pastoral, 1991.

Baldwin, Anna, and Sarah Hutton, eds. *Platonism and the English Imagination.* Cambridge: Cambridge University Press, 1994.

Balthasar, Hans Urs von. *The Moment of Christian Witness.* Translated by Richard Beckley. San Francisco: Ignatius, 1994.

Barfield, Owen. *Poetic Diction: A Study in Meaning.* Middletown, CT: Wesleyan University Press, 1973.

———. *Saving the Appearances: A Study in Idolatry.* Middletown, CT: Wesleyan University Press, 1988.

————. *What Coleridge Thought*. Oxford: Barfield, 2014.

Barker, Margaret. *The Great Angel: A Study of Israel's Second God*. Louisville, KY: Westminster John Knox, 1992.

————. *The Lost Prophet: The Book of Enoch and its Influence on Christianity*. Sheffield, UK: Sheffield Phoenix, 1998.

————. *Temple Themes in Christian Worship*. London: T. & T. Clark, 2007.

Becker, Matthew L. *Fundamental Theology: A Protestant Perspective*. London: T. & T. Clark, 2015.

Beeley, Christopher A. "Christ and Human Flourishing in Patristic Theology." *Pro Ecclesia* 25, no. 2 (2016) 126–53.

Behr, John. *The Nicene Faith, Part One. The Formation of Christian Theology, Vol. 2*. Crestwood, NY: St. Vladimir's Seminary Press, 2004.

————. *The Nicene Faith, Part Two. The Formation of Christian Theology, Vol. 2*. Crestwood, NY: St. Vladimir's Seminary Press, 2004.

————. *The Way to Nicaea. The Formation of Christian Theology, Vol. 1*. Crestwood, NY: St. Vladimir's Seminary Press, 2001.

Biggar, Nigel. *Between Kin and Cosmopolis: An Ethic of the Nation*. Didsbury Lectures series. Eugene, OR: Cascade, 2014.

Binder, Donald D. *Into the Temple Courts: The Place of Synagogues in the Second Temple Period*. Atlanta: SBL, 1999.

Bloomfield, Morton W. *Piers Plowman as a Fourteenth-century Apocalypse*. New Brunswick, NJ: Rutgers University Press, 1962.

Blunt, John Henry. *The Annotated Book of Common Prayer: Being an Historical, Ritual, and Theological Commentary on the Devotional System of The Church of England*. London: Rivingtons, 1866.

Boersma, Hans. *Heavenly Participation: The Weaving of a Sacramental Tapestry*. Grand Rapids: Eerdmans, 2011.

Boethius. *The Theological Tractates and The Consolation of Philosophy*. Translated by H. F. Stewart and E. K. Rand. Cambridge: Harvard University Press, 1946.

Bouyer, Louis. *The Christian Mystery: From Pagan Myth to Christian Mysticism*. Translated by Illtyd Trethowan. 1989. Reprint. London: T. & T. Clark, 2004.

Bradshaw, Paul F. "Difficulties in Doing Liturgical Theology." *Pacifica* 11, no. 2 (1998) 181–94.

Brisson, Luc. *Plato the Myth Maker*. Edited and translated by Gerard Naddaf. Chicago: University of Chicago Press, 1998.

Brown, David. *God and Grace of Body: Sacrament in Ordinary*. Oxford: Oxford University Press, 2007.

Brown, Peter. *The Body and Society: Men, Women, and Sexual Renunciation in Early Christianity*. New York: Columbia University Press, 2008.

Brunk, Timothy. "A Holy and Living Sacrifice," *Liturgical Ministry* 18 (2009) 59–67.

Bucur, Bogdan Gabriel. *Angelomorphic Pneumatology: Clement of Alexandria and Other Early Christian Witnesses*. Supplements to *Vigiliae Christianae*. Leiden: Brill, 2009.

Burkert, Walter. *Homo Necans: The Anthropology of Ancient Greek Sacrificial Ritual and Myth*. Translated by Peter Bing. Berkeley: University of California Press, 1983.

————. *Ancient Mystery Cults*. Cambridge: Harvard University Press, 1987.

————. *Greek Religion*. Translated by John Raffan. Cambridge: Harvard University Press, 1985.

Burrell, David. *Creation and the God of Abraham*. Cambridge: Cambridge University Press, 2010.

Caldecott, Stratford: *The Radiance of Being: Dimensions of Cosmic Christianity*. Tacoma, WA: Angelico, 2013.

Canty, Aaron. "Balancing Letter and Spirit." *The Living Church*, February 27, 2011.

Carr, David M. *The Formation of the Hebrew Bible: A New Reconstruction*. Oxford: Oxford University Press, 2011.

Casel, Odo. *The Mystery of Christian Worship and Other Writings*. Translated by I. T. Hale and edited by Burkhard Neunheuser. New York: Herder & Herder, 1999.

Cassirer, Ernst. *The Platonic Renaissance in England*. Translated by James P. Pettergrove. Austin, TX: University of Texas Press, 1953.

Clarahan, Mary Ann. "Mystagogy and Mystery." *Worship* 83, no. 6 (2009) 502–23.

Congar, Yves. *At the Heart of Christian Worship: Liturgical Essays of Yves Congar*. Translated and edited by Paul Philibert. Collegeville, MN: Liturgical, 2010.

Coogan, Michael D., and Mark S. Smith, eds. and trans. *Stories from Ancient Canaan*. 2nd ed. Louisville, KY: Westminster John Knox, 2012.

Cook, Bernard, and Gary Macy. *Christian Symbol and Ritual: An Introduction*. Oxford: Oxford University Press, 2005.

Daly, Robert. *Sacrifice Unveiled: The True Meaning of Christian Sacrifice*. London: T. & T. Clark, 2009.

DeHaan, M. R. *The Romance of Redemption: Studies in the Book of Ruth*. Grand Rapids: Kregel, 1995.

Dennett, Daniel C. *Breaking the Spell: Religion as a Natural Phenomenon*. New York: Penguin, 2006.

Derrida, Jacques. *Writing and Difference*. Translated by Alan Bass. Chicago: University of Chicago Press, 1978.

Dodds, Eric R. *The Greeks and the Irrational*. Berkeley: University of California Press, 1951.

Douglas, Mary. *Natural Symbols: Explorations in Cosmology*. 1970. Reprint. New York: Routledge, 2003.

———. *Leviticus as Literature*. Oxford: Oxford University Press, 1999.

Ellul, Jacques. *The Meaning of the City*. Translated by Dennis Pardee. 1970. Reprint. Eugene, OR: Wipf & Stock, 2011.

Emminghaus, Johannes H. *The Eucharist: Essence, Form, Celebration*. Translated by Linda M. Maloney. 1972. Reprint. Collegeville, MN: Liturgical, 1997.

Evagrius. *Evagrius, Kephalaia Gnostika: A New Translation of the Unreformed Text from the Syriac*. Translated by Ilaria L. E. Ramelli. Atlanta: SBL, 2015.

———. *The Praktikos & Chapters on Prayer*. Translated by John Eudes Bamberger. Kalamazoo, MI: Cistercian, 1981.

Evans, Nancy. "Diotima and Demeter as Mystagogues in Plato's Symposium." *Hypatia* 21, no. 2 (2006) 1–27.

Fagerberg, David W. "The Cost of Understanding Schmemann in the West." Online: http://www.ancientfaith.com/specials/svs_liturgical_symposium/the_cost_of_understanding_schmemann_in_the_west.

———. "Divine Liturgy, Divine Love; Towards a New Understanding of Sacrifice in Christian Worship." In *The Hermeneutic of Continuity: Christ, Kingdom, and Creation. Letter and Spirit, Volume 3*, edited by Scott Hahn and David Scott, 95–112. Steubenville, OH: St. Paul Center for Biblical Theology, 2007.

———. *On Liturgical Asceticism*. Washington, DC: The Catholic University of America Press, 2013.

———. "Theologia Prima: The Liturgical Mystery and the Mystery of God." In *The Authority of Mystery: The Word of God and the People of God. Letter and Spirit, Volume 2*, edited by Scott Hahn and David Scott, 55–68. Steubenville, OH: St. Paul Center for Biblical Theology, 2006.

Farrer, Austin. *The Glass of Vision*. Westminster, London: Dacre Press, 1948.

Fleischaker, Mary Frances. "Mystagogy and Liturgical Synesthesia: An Inter-Disciplinary Excursion." *Liturgical Ministry* 18, no. 3 (2009) 126–32.

Fletcher-Louis, Crispin. *Jesus Monotheism Volume 1: Christological Origins: The Emerging Consensus and Beyond*. Eugene, OR: Wipf and Stock, 2015.

Flipper, Joseph S. *Between Apocalypse and Eschaton: History and Eternity in Henri de Lubac*. Minneapolis: Fortress, 2015.

Fragomeni, Richard N. "Wounded in Extraordinary Depths: Towards a Contemporary Mystagogia." In *A Promise of Presence: Studies in Honor of David N. Power, OMI*, edited by Michael Downey and Richard Fragomeni, 115–37. Washington, DC: Pastoral, 1992.

Frei, Hans W. *The Eclipse of Biblical Narrative: A Study in Eighteenth- and Nineteenth-Century Hermeneutics*. New Haven: Yale University Press, 1974.

Gadamer, Hans-Georg. *Truth and Method*. New York: Bloomsbury Academic, 2013.

Garrigan, Siobhán. *Beyond Ritual: Sacramental Theology after Habermas*. Burlington, VT: Ashgate, 2004.

Geldhof, Joris. "Liturgy as Theological Norm: Getting Acquainted with 'Liturgical Theology.'" *Neue Zeitschrift Für Systematische Theologie Und Religionsphilosophie* 52, no. 2 (2010) 155–76.

———. *Revelation, Reason and Reality: Theological Encounters with Jaspers, Schelling and Baader*. Studies in Philosophical Theology. Leuven: Peeters, 2007.

Gerlach, Matthew Thomas. "Lex Orandi, Lex Legendi: A Correlation of the Roman Canon and the Fourfold Sense of Scripture." PhD Diss., Marquette University, 2011.

Gerson, Lloyd P. *From Plato to Platonism*. Ithaca, NY: Cornell University Press, 2013.

———. *Knowing Persons: A Study in Plato*. Oxford: Oxford University Press, 2003.

Getcha, Job. "From Master to Disciple: The Notion of 'Liturgical Theology' in Fr Kiprian Kern and Fr Alexander Schmemann." *St. Vladimir's Theological Quarterly* 53, no. 2–3 (2009) 251–72.

Gignilliat, Mark S. "God Speaks Hebrew: The Hebrew Text and Septuagint in the Search for the Christian Bible." *Pro Ecclesia* 25, no. 2 (2016) 154–72.

Graham, David. "Defending Biblical Literalism: Augustine on the Literal Sense." *Pro Ecclesia* 25, no. 2 (2016) 173–99.

Gray, John. *Straw Dogs: Thoughts on Humans and Other Animals*. 2002. Reprint. New York: Farrar, Straus and Giroux, 2003.

Green, Alberto R. W. *The Storm-God in the Ancient Near East*. Biblical and Judaic Studies Volume 8. Winona Lake, IN: Eisenbrauns, 2003.

Gregory, Alan P. R. *Coleridge and the Conservative Imagination*. Macon, GA: Mercer University Press, 2003.

Gregory Nazianzus. *On God and Christ: The Five Theological Orations and Two Letters to Cledonius*. Translated by Frederick Williams and Lionel Wickham. Yonkers, NY: St. Vladimir's Seminary Press, 2002.

Gruenwald, Ithamar. *Rituals and Ritual Theory in Ancient Israel*. Atlanta: SBL, 2010.

Hadot, Pierre. *Philosophy as a Way of Life: Spiritual Exercises from Socrates to Foucault*. Malden, MA: Blackwell, 1995.

———. *What is Ancient Philosophy?* Translated by Michael Chase. Cambridge: Harvard University Press, 2002.

Hahn, Scott. "Worship in the Word: Toward a Liturgical Hermeneutic." In *Reading Salvation: Word, Worship, and the Mysteries. Letter and Spirit, Volume 1*, edited by Scott Hahn, 101–36. Steubenville, OH: St. Paul Center for Biblical Theology, 2005.

Haidt, Jonathan. *The Righteous Mind: Why Good People are Divided by Politics and Religion*. New York: Vintage, 2012.

Halbertal, Moshe. *On Sacrifice*. Princeton: Princeton University Press, 2012.

Hankey, Wayne J., and Douglas Hedley, eds. *Deconstructing Radical Orthodoxy: Postmodern Theology, Rhetoric and Truth*. Burlington, VT: Ashgate, 2005.

Haran, Menahem. *Temples and Temple-Service in Ancient Israel: An Inquiry into the Character of Cult Phenomena and the Historical Setting of the Priestly School*. 1995. Reprint. Winona Lake, IN: Eisenbrauns, 1985.

Hart, David Bentley. *The Experience of God: Being, Consciousness, Bliss*. New Haven: Yale University Press, 2013.

———. "A Gift Exceeding Every Debt: An Eastern Orthodox Appreciation of Anselm's *Cur Deus Homo*." *Pro Ecclesia* 8, no. 3 (1998) 333–48.

Hebblethwaite, Brian, and Douglas Hedley, eds. *The Human Person in God's World: Studies to Commemorate the Austin Farrer Centenary*. London: SCM, 2006.

Hedley, Douglas. *Coleridge, Philosophy and Religion: Aids to Reflection and the Mirror of the Spirit*. Cambridge: Cambridge University Press, 2000.

———. *Living Forms of the Imagination*. London: T. & T. Clark, 2008.

———. *Sacrifice Imagined: Violence, Atonement, and the Sacred*. New York: Continuum, 2011.

———. *The Iconic Imagination*. New York: Bloomsbury Academic, 2016.

Hedley, Douglas, and Sarah Hutton, eds. *Platonism at the Origins of Modernity: Studies on Platonism and Early Modern Philosophy*. 2008. Reprint. Dordrecht: Springer, 2010.

Hoff, Johannes. *The Analogical Turn: Rethinking Modernity with Nicholas of Cusa*. Interventions. Grand Rapids: Eerdmans, 2013.

———. "The Rise and Fall of the Kantian Paradigm of Modern Theology." In *Grandeur of Reason: Religion, Tradition and Universalism*, edited by Conor Cunningham and Peter Candler 167–96. Veritas. London: SCM, 2010.

Holman, Susan R. *The Hungry Are Dying: Beggars and Bishops in Roman Cappadocia*. Oxford: Oxford University Press, 2001.

Hoskins, Paul M. *Jesus as the Fulfillment of the Temple in the Gospel of John*. Paternoster Biblical Monographs. Eugene, OR: Wipf & Stock, 2006.

Hovey, Craig. *To Share in the Body: A Theology of Martyrdom for Today's Church*. Grand Rapids: Brazos, 2008.

Hughes, Kathleen. *Saying Amen: A Mystagogy of Sacrament*. Chicago: Liturgy Training, 1999.

Hyde, Lewis. *The Gift: Creativity and the Artist in the Modern World*. 1979. Reprint. New York: Vintage, 2007.

The Hymnal 1982. New York: Church Publishing, 1985.

Inge, William Ralph. *The Platonic Tradition in English Religious Thought*. London: Longmans, Greed and Co., 1926.

Jacobsen, Thorkild. *The Treasures of Darkness: A History of Mesopotamian Religion*. New Haven: Yale University Press, 1976.

Janowitz, Naomi. *Icons of Power: Ritual Practices in Late Antiquity. Magic in History.* University Park, PA: The Pennsylvania State University Press, 2002.

Jennings, Nathan G. "Contemplating the Mystery: Liturgical Theology as Retrieval of Christian Realism." *Questions Liturgiques* 96, no. 1 (2015) 8–19.

———. "Divine Economy, Divine Liturgy: Liturgical Theology as a Retrieval of Figural Interpretation," *Radical Orthodoxy: Theology, Philosophy, Politics* 2, no. 1 (2014) 90–117.

———. *Theology as Ascetic Act: Disciplining Christian Discourse*. New York: Lang, 2010.

Jenson, Philip Peter. *Graded Holiness: A Key to the Priestly Conception of the World*. Journal for the Study of the Old Testament Supplement Series 106. Sheffield, UK: Sheffield Academic Press, 1992.

Jenson, Robert W. "Gratia non tollit naturam sed perficit." *Pro Ecclesia* 25, no. 1 (2016) 44–52.

Johnson, Dru. *Knowledge by Ritual: A Biblical Prolegomenon to Sacramental Theology*. Winona Lake, IN: Eisenbrauns, 2016.

Kavanagh, Aidan. *On Liturgical Theology*. Collegeville, MN: Liturgical, 1992.

Keller, Mara Lynn. "The Ritual Path of Initiation into the Eleusinian Mysteries." *Rosicrucian Digest* 2 (2009) 28–42.

Kenney, John Peter. *Mystical Monotheism: A Study in Ancient Platonic Theology*. 1991. Reprint. Eugene, OR: Wipf & Stock, 2010.

Kerr, Alan R. *The Temple of Jesus' Body: The Temple Theme in the Gospel of John*. Library of New Testament Studies. Sheffield, UK: Sheffield Academic Press, 2002.

Kerr, Fergus. "Tradition and Reason: Two Uses of Reason, Critical and Contemplative." *International Journal Of Systematic Theology* 6, no. 1 (2004) 37–49.

King, Peter. *Private Dwelling: Contemplating the Use of Housing*. London: Routledge, 2004.

Kinzer, Mark. "Temple Christology in the Gospel of John." *Society of Biblical Literature Seminar Papers* 37, no. 1 (1998) 447–64.

Klawans, Jonathan. *Purity, Sacrifice, and the Temple: Symbolism and Supersessionism in the Study of Ancient Judaism*. Oxford: Oxford University Press, 2006.

Klingbeil, Gerald A. *Bridging the Gap: Ritual and Ritual Texts in the Bible*. Winona Lake, IN: Eisenbrauns, 2007.

Koester, Craig R. "Hebrews." *The Anchor Bible: A New Translation with Introduction and Commentary, Volume 36*. New York: Doubleday, 2001.

Lathrop, Gordon. *Holy Ground: A Liturgical Cosmology*. 2003. Reprint. Minneapolis: Fortress, 2009.

———. *Holy People: A Liturgical Ecclesiology*. 1999. Reprint. Minneapolis: Fortress, 2006.

———. *Holy Things: A Liturgical Theology*. 1993. Reprint. Minneapolis: Fortress, 1998.

Lawrence, D. H. *Aaron's Rod*. New York: Seltzer, 1922.

Legaspi, Michael C. *The Death of Scripture and the Rise of Biblical Studies*. Oxford Studies in Historical Theology. Oxford: Oxford University Press, 2010.

Leithart, Peter. *Gratitude: An Intellectual History*. Waco, TX: Baylor University Press, 2014.

Levenson, Jon D. *Creation and the Persistence of Evil: The Jewish Drama of Divine Omnipotence*. Princeton: Princeton University Press, 1988.

———. *The Death and Resurrection of the Beloved Son: The Transformation of Child Sacrifice in Judaism and Christianity*. New Haven: Yale University Press, 1993.

———. *Sinai and Zion: An Entry into the Jewish Bible*. New York: Harper and Row, 1987.

Levering, Matthew. *Christ's Fulfillment of Torah and Temple: Salvation According to Thomas Aquinas*. Notre Dame, IN: University of Notre Dame Press, 2002.

———. *Sacrifice and Community: Jewish Offering and Christian Eucharist. Illuminations: Theory and Religion*. Malden, MA: Blackwell, 2005.

Louth, Andrew. *Denys the Areopagite*. Outstanding Christian Thinkers. New York: Bloomsbury Academic, 2002.

———. "Platonism in the Middle English Mystics." In *Platonism and the English Imagination*, edited by Anna Baldwin and Sarah Hutton, 52-64. Cambridge: Cambridge University Press, 1994.

Lothes Biviano, Erin. *The Paradox of Christian Sacrifice: The Loss of Self, the Gift of Self*. New York: Herder & Herder, 2007.

Lubac, Henri de. *Corpus Mysticum: The Eucharist and the Church in the Middle Ages*. Translated by Gemma Simmons, CJ, Richard Price, and Christopher Stephens. Edited by Laurence Price Hemming and Susan Frank Parsons. Notre Dame, IN: University of Notre Dame Press, 2007.

———. *Medieval Exegesis: The Four Senses of Scripture*, Vol. 1. Translated by Mark Sebanc. Grand Rapids: Eerdmans, 1998.

———. *Medieval Exegesis: The Four Senses of Scripture*, Vol. 2. Translated by E. M. Maclerowski. Grand Rapids: Eerdmans, 2000.

———. *Medieval Exegesis: The Four Senses of Scripture*, Vol. 3. Translated by E. M. Maclerowski. Grand Rapids: Eerdmans, 2009.

———. *The Mystery of the Supernatural*. New York: Crossroad, 1998.

———. *Three Jesuits Speak: Yves De Montcheuil, Charles Nicolet, Jean Zupan*. San Francisco: Ignatius, 1987.

Mazza, Enrico. *Mystagogy: A Theology of Liturgy in the Patristic Age*. Translated by Matthew J. O'Connell. New York: Pueblo, 1989.

McGowan, Andrew B. "Eucharist and Sacrifice: Cultic Tradition and Transformation in Early Christian Ritual Meals." In *Mahl und religiöse Identität im frühen Christentum: Meals and Religious Identity in Early Christianity*, edited by Matthias Klinghardt and Hal Taussig, 191–206. Tübingen: Francke, 2012.

———. "Rehashing the Leftovers of Idols: Cyprian and Early Christian Constructions of Sacrifice." In *Religious Competition in the Third Century CE: Jews, Christians, and the Greco-Roman World*, edited by Jordan D. Rosenblum et al., 68–79. Göttingen: Vandenhoeck and Ruprecht, 2014.

Meeks, Wayne. *The First Urban Christians: The Social World of the Apostle Paul*. 2nd ed. New Haven: Yale University Press, 1983.

Milbank, John. *Theology and Social Theory: Beyond Secular Reason*. 2nd ed. Malden, MA: Blackwell, 2006.

Miller, Patricia Cox. *The Corporeal Imagination: Signifying the Holy in Late Ancient Christianity*. Divinations: Rereading Late Ancient Religion. 2009. Reprint. Philadelphia: University of Pennsylvania Press, 2016.

Moore, Stephen D., and Yvonne Sherwood. *The Invention of the Biblical Scholar: A Critical Manifesto*. Minneapolis: Fortress, 2011.

Muirhead, John H. *The Platonic Tradition in Anglo-Saxon Philosophy: Studies in the History of Idealism in England and America*. New York: Allen and Unwin, 1965.

Muller, Jerry Z., ed. *Conservatism: An Anthology of Social and Political Thought from David Hume to the Present*. Princeton: Princeton University Press, 1997.

Mumford, Lewis. "What Is a City?" In *The City Reader*, edited by Richard T. LeGates and Frederic Stout, 110–14. 6th ed. New York: Routledge, 2016.

Nicholas of Cusa. *Metaphysical Speculations, Volume 2*. Translated by Jasper Hopkins. Minneapolis: Banning, 2000.

Oakeshott, Michael. *Rationalism in Politics and Other Essays*. London: Methuen, 1984.

Osborn, Eric. *Irenaeus of Lyons*. Cambridge: Cambridge University Press, 2001.

Peterson, Brian K. "What Happened on 'The Night'? Judas, God and the Importance of Liturgical Ambiguity." *Pro Ecclesia* 20, no. 4 (2011) 363–83.

Parry, Robin A. *The Biblical Cosmos: A Pilgrim's Guide to the Weird and Wonderful World of the Bible*. Illustrated by Hannah Parry. Eugene, OR: Cascade, 2014.

Patrides, C. A. and Joseph Wittreich, eds. *The Apocalypse in English Renaissance Thought and Literature: Patterns, Antecedents and Repercussions*. Manchester: Manchester University Press, 1984.

Pott, Thomas. *Byzantine Liturgical Reform: A Study of Liturgical Change in the Byzantine Tradition*. Crestwood, NY: St. Vladimir's Seminary Press, 2010.

Price, Charles P., and Louis Weil. *Liturgy for Living*. Rev. ed. Harrisburg, PA: Morehouse, 2000.

Pritchard, James B., ed. *The Ancient Near East, Volume I: An Anthology of Texts and Pictures*. Princeton: Princeton University Press, 1958.

———, ed. *The Ancient Near East, Volume II: A New Anthology of Texts and Pictures*. Princeton: Princeton University Press, 1975.

Pseudo-Dionysius. *Pseudo-Dionysius: The Complete Works*. Classics of Western Spirituality. Translated by Colm Luibheid. New York: Paulist, 1987.

Purcell, Brendan. *From Big Bang to Big Mystery: Human Origins in the Light of Creation and Evolution*. Hyde Park, NY: New City, 2012.

Ramshaw, Gail. *Christian Worship: 100,000 Sundays of Symbols and Rituals*. Minneapolis: Fortress, 2009.

———. *Treasures Old and New: Images in the Lectionary*. Minneapolis: Augsburg Fortress, 2002.

Ricoeur, Paul. *Interpretation Theory: Discourse and the Surplus of Meaning*. Fort Worth: Texas Christian University Press, 1976.

Ross, Allen P. *Recalling the Hope of Glory: Biblical Worship from the Garden to the New Creation*. Grand Rapids: Kregel, 2006.

Rowland, Christopher. *The Open Heaven: A Study of Apocalyptic in Judaism and Early Christianity*. 1982. Reprint. Eugene, OR: Wipf & Stock, 2002.

Saliers, Don E. *Worship as Theology: Foretaste of Glory Divine*. Nashville: Abingdon,1994.

Sallustius, Demophilus, Proclus. *Sallust, On the Gods and the World. The Pythagoric Sentences of Demophilus. Five Hymns*. Translated by Thomas Taylor. Los Angeles: Philosophical Research Society, 1976.

Schmemann, Alexander. *The Eucharist: Sacrament of the Kingdom*. Crestwood, NY: St. Vladimir's Seminary Press, 1988.

———. *For the Life of the World: Sacraments and Orthodoxy*. Crestwood, NY: St. Vladimir's Seminary Press, 1973.

———. *Introduction to Liturgical Theology*. Crestwood, NY: St. Vladimir's Seminary Press, 1975.

Scully, Jason. "Angelic Pneumatology in the Egyptian Desert: The Role of the Angels and the Holy Spirit in Evagrian Asceticism." *Journal of Early Christian Studies* 19, no. 2 (2011) 287–305.

Searle, Mark. *Called to Participate: Theological, Ritual, and Social Perspectives.* Collegeville, MN: Liturgical, 2006.

Serra, Dominic E. "The Roman Canon: The Theological Significance of Its Structure and Syntax." *Ecclesia Orans* no. 20 (2003) 99–128.

Slater, Gary. *C. S. Pierce and the Nested Continua of Religious Interpretation.* Oxford: Oxford University Press, 2015.

Snell, Daniel C, ed. *A Companion to the Ancient Near East.* Blackwell Companions to the Ancient World. Malden, MA: Blackwell, 2005.

Steiner, George. *Real Presences.* Chicago: University of Chicago Press, 1989.

Stephenson, Barry. *Ritual: A Very Short Introduction.* Oxford: Oxford University Press, 2015.

Stuhlman, Byron D. *A Good and Joyful Thing: The Evolution of the Eucharistic Prayer.* New York: Church Publishing, 2000.

Taft, Robert F. *Beyond East and West: Problems in Liturgical Understanding.* Rome: Pontifical Oriental Institute, 2001.

———. "The Liturgical Year: Studies, Prospects, Reflections." *Worship* 55, no. 1 (1981) 2–23.

Tanner, Kathryn. *God and Creation in Christian Theology: Tyranny or Empowerment?* Minneapolis: Fortress, 2005.

———. *Jesus, Humanity and the Trinity: A Brief Systematic Theology.* Minneapolis: Fortress, 2001.

———. *Theories of Culture: A New Agenda for Theology.* Guides to Theological Inquiry. Minneapolis: Augsburg Fortress, 1997.

Taylor, Charles. *The Language Animal: The Full Shape of the Human Linguistic Capacity.* Cambridge: Harvard University Press, 2016.

———. *A Secular Age.* Cambridge: Harvard University Press, 2007.

———. "Two Theories of Modernity." *The Hastings Center Report* 25, no. 2 (1995) 24–33.

Taylor, Jeremy. *Jeremy Taylor, Selected Works.* Edited by Thomas K. Carroll. New York: Paulist, 1990.

Thornton, Martin. *Christian Proficiency.* 1988. Reprint. Eugene, OR: Wipf & Stock, 2010.

———. *Pastoral Theology: A Reorientation.* 1958. Reprint. Eugene, OR: Wipf & Stock, 2010.

Tolkien, J. R. R. "Leaf by Niggle." In *Tree and Leaf*, 91–119. New York: HarperCollins, 2001.

———. *The Silmarillion.* 2nd ed. Edited by Christopher Tolkien. New York: Houghton Mifflin, 2001.

Tyson, Paul. *Returning to Reality: Christian Platonism for Our Times.* Kalos Series 2. Eugene, OR: Cascade, 2014.

Upton, Charles. *Folk Metaphysics: Mystical Meanings in Traditional Folk Songs and Spirituals.* San Rafael, CA: Sophia Perennis, 2008.

Uždavinys, Algis. *Philosophy as a Rite of Rebirth: From Ancient Egypt to Neoplatonism.* Westbury, UK: The Prometheus Trust, 2008.

———. *Philosophy and Theurgy in Late Antiquity.* San Rafael, CA: Sophia Perennis, 2010.

van de Wiele, Tarah. "What Rights Get Wrong about Justice for Orphans: An Old Testament Challenge to a Modern Ideology." *Studies in Christian Ethics* 29, no. 1 (2016) 69–83.

Vogel, Dwight W., ed. *Primary Sources of Liturgical Theology: A Reader*. Collegeville, MN: Liturgical, 2000.

Webb, Stephen H. "Gratitude: An Intellectual History." *The Christian Century* 131, no. 9 (April 30, 2014) 47–48.

Weil, Louis. *Liturgical Sense: The Logic of Rite*. New York: Seabury, 2013.

Whaling, Frank. "The Development of the Word 'Theology.'" *Scottish Journal of Theology* 34 (1981) 289–312.

Wilken, Robert L. *The Spirit of Early Christian Thought: Seeking the Face of God*. New Haven: Yale University Press, 2003.

Wills, Garry. *Font of Life: Ambrose, Augustine, and the Mystery of Baptism*. Oxford: Oxford University Press, 2012.

Wood, Susan K. *Spiritual Exegesis and the Church in the Theology of Henri de Lubac*. 1998. Reprint. Eugene, OR: Wipf & Stock, 2010.

Zimmerman, Joyce Ann. *Liturgy as Language of Faith*. Lanham, MD: University Press of America, 1988.

———. *Liturgy and Hermeneutics*. Collegeville, MN: Liturgical, 1999.

Zizioulas, John D. *Being as Communion: Studies in Personhood and the Church*. Crestwood, NY: St. Vladimir's Seminary Press, 1985.

Subject/Name Index

Scripture Index